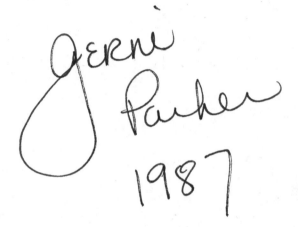

Jerni
Parker
1987

The NATURE of DEMOCRACY FREEDOM and REVOLUTION

BY HERBERT APTHEKER

INTERNATIONAL PUBLISHERS

NEW YORK

For Bettina

ISBN 0–7178–0137–3
Library of Congress Catalog Number: 67–29076
Manufactured in the United States of America

Contents

I. Freedom in History

Let us begin with two brief sentences taken from quite different authors. One comes from Christopher Caudwell, killed while yet a youth, fighting fascism in Spain. "Liberty," wrote* this martyred Communist, "does seem to me the most important of all generalized goods." The other comes from a liberal American scholar, Ralph S. Brown, Jr., and appears in the midst of what is generally an extremely valuable study of *Loyalty and Security: Employment Tests in the United States* (1958): "Communism denies freedom and attempts to destroy it."

Imperative, I think, is an awareness of freedom as an historical process; as something still in the course of being achieved, and as something, therefore, that must be viewed within its time and place and social context.

We may illustrate this by considering some of the best known and most frequently quoted writings of the three pre-eminent English-speaking libertarians: John Milton, Thomas Jefferson, and John Stuart Mill. Surely, none has been more frequently appealed to in justification of an abstract freedom than these three. An examination of the body of their writings, however—and not the culling of this

*Studies and Further Studies in a Dying Culture, by Christopher Caudwell, N. Y., 1958, p. 193.

or that sentence—will show that all three were battlers for the advancement of human freedom in the concrete, in the course of their own passionate participation in specific historic epochs and for specific historic purposes. While these reflect the limitations of themselves and of their writings, they also reflect their greatness, and made possible their greatness, their actual contributions to the forward march of humanity—in real life, not in the abstract.

John Milton

The paragraph in Milton most commonly quoted is taken from his *Areopagitica* and, with spelling modernized, reads as follows:

"And though all the winds of doctrine were let loose to play upon the earth, so Truth be in the field, we do injuriously by licensing and prohibiting to misdoubt her strength. Let her and Falsehood grapple; who ever knew Truth put to the worse in a free and open encounter?"

One is moved at once to query: *when* did Truth and Falsehood meet each other "in a free and open encounter"? Especially where the matter under debate was significant and the socio-political order was exploitative and class-divided? But let us not pose 20th-century questions for our 17th-century giant. Let us rather look at him in his century and in his homeland, and in this particular book, and see what it is he means.

The sentences just quoted come from pages 51-52 of the edition I have used (Oxford Uni-

versity Press, 1894). The work itself, first printed
in 1644, was a contribution to the debates in
an England in civil war. Milton was an adherent
of the Independents in that conflict, and they,
battling for the Truth, as they saw it, perse-
cuted Catholics; prohibited the Episcopalian
worship; punished anti-trinitarians; and burned
books held to be blasphemous. What, then, is
the point of Milton's pamphlet subtitled "For
the Liberty of Unlicensed Printing," and why
does he appear, in the quoted passage, to be
urging freedom for "all the winds of doctrine"?
If one knows the occasion of the essay and
the party of its author, it is possible to begin
to answer this question. Then, one needs but
read on in Milton. For two pages after the
quoted sentences, appears a paragraph not often
quoted, but without which the first can be,
as it often has been, utterly misunderstood.
Here, again, is Milton:

"Yet if all cannot be of one mind, as who
looks they should be, this doubtless is more
wholesome, more prudent, and more Christian:
that many may be tolerated rather than all
compelled. I mean not tolerated Popery and
open superstition which as it extirpates all
religions and civil supremacies, so itself should
be extirpated, provided first that all charitable
and compassionate means be used to win and
regain the weak and misled; that also which
is impious or evil absolutely either against
faith or manners no law can possibly permit,
that intends not to unlaw itself; but *those
neighboring differences, or rather indifferences,
are what I speak of*, whether in some point of

doctrine or of discipline, which though they may be many, yet need not interrupt the unity of Spirit, if we could but find among us the bond of peace. In the meanwhile, if anyone would write, and *bring his helpful hand to the slow-moving Reformation,* which we labor under, if Truth have spoken to him before others, or but seemed at least to speak, who has so bejesuited us that we should trouble that man with asking license *to do so worthy a deed?*" (Italics added.)

The partisanship of Milton is perfectly clear; and the extreme limitations among "the winds of doctrine" that he wishes to "let loose" are also clear. The advance is present; the struggle against feudalism and in favor of the Reformation, on behalf of which Milton writes and brings out argumentation urging the enhancement of freedom—but not freedom in the abstract. Rather, freedom in terms of the 17th-century, Protestant, bourgeois - revolutionary efforts in England.

Thomas Jefferson

Frequently, Jefferson, too, is presented as the advocate of an abstracted freedom. Thus, the distinguished Justice William O. Douglas, in his splendid attack upon reaction, *The Right of the People* (N.Y., 1958), quotes Jefferson, "Truth is the proper and sufficient antagonist to error," and he sums up his understanding of "the Jeffersonian faith," by declaring it held that if mankind were "allowed unfettered liberty to accumulate knowledge and in the process even to wallow in trash, if they like, they will acquire the wisdom and ability to manage all of the perplexing and teasing problems of each generation." Similarly, another quotation very often presented from Jefferson runs this way: "If a book be false in its facts, disprove them; if false in its reasoning, refute it. But for God's sake, let us freely hear both sides."

Queries immediately occur, once again, particularly in terms of experiences gained through living several generations after Jefferson. For example: are there but two sides, and are there no shadings of that which is true and that which is false in many sides of all kinds of disputes? And again, notice Jefferson's confident Age-of-Reason assumption that through "reasoning" and the presentation of "facts" one could arrive at the "truth"—but what then? That is to say, does not Jefferson assume that, having so arrived, the debate is closed and on the basis of the ascertainment of truth, action in accordance therewith necessarily follows?

It is necessary, again, if one is to grasp Jeffersonianism, and gain what light it may shed upon the problem of human freedom, to see it and its creator in their time—18th and early 19th-century America—in the throes of bringing about and maintaining a great bourgeois-democratic, anti-colonial revolution. In doing this, one can better, more fully, understand the matter. For example, does it not help to know that the hand which wrote the Declaration of Independence also wrote advertisements for fugitive slaves? Does it not help to understand the matter, to know that when the Declaration said all men are created equal, it meant men and not women? And, that it meant some men but not all—for living then in the rebellious colonies were 650,000 slaves and 250,000 indentured servants and 300,000 Indians; of this 40 per cent of the total population, all the men, let alone the women, were excluded from considerations of equality, as they were from any role in the exercise of "popular sovereignty."

This is not said in any spirit of muckraking, or of exposing the clay feet of Jefferson, the idol. No man is to be idolized; but if one were forced to select an idol among human beings, he could not do very much better than select Thomas Jefferson. These things are said in a spirit of insisting upon that truth, to whose further exposition Jefferson devoted his life; they are said in an effort to get at the reality of the concept of human freedom, for the realization of which Jefferson did so much.

And when we speak this way, in terms of the realities of history, in terms of the realities of the social orders within which all of us live and all in the past have lived, there remain other considerations relevant to Jefferson's life and beliefs to be observed. Thus, Jefferson was, of course, a foremost revolutionary leader, and had momentous political responsibilities in that capacity; he was, for example, a member of the Continental Congress and he was a Governor of revolutionary Virginia.

Among the responsibilities which Jefferson faced with all the Founding Fathers was that of carrying the Revolution through successfully and of preserving it after military success. In that regard, one of the critical problems before the revolutionary founders was the handling of counter-revolutionaries, the so-called Tories. There were, during the Revolution, perhaps 600,000 to 700,000 people who were loyal to the King, and of these, many thousands were active in asserting that loyalty. From them, the Revolutionists, including Jefferson, took away the right to vote or hold office; they were forbidden to teach or to preach or to practice any profession. Those who were wealthy, found their property confiscated (without trial); many suffered serious physical harm; many were jailed (without trial) and served long years of forced labor; some were executed (including some without trial); the presses of the Tories were confiscated; over 100,000 of them were forced into exile. And most of the disabilities of the Tories persisted until six or seven years after the last shot had been fired; some of them, especially involving property, never were made good.

Here was a living question of all kinds of rights—press, speech, assemblage, suffrage, due process of law, etc.—and they were deliberately denied scores of thousands of people for some 12 or 13 years. But if there is one word denouncing or deprecating this in the writings of Jefferson or Madison or Monroe or Henry or Washington, or the Adamses, this writer, after prolonged searching, has failed to uncover it. Here was a concrete case where during a bourgeois-democratic revolution, in order to extend the liberties of a large number of people, heretofore oppressed and subjugated, it was necessary to smash institutions upholding such subjugation and to inhibit the liberties of others.

One further instance out of the life and times of Jefferson: All know of the Alien and Sedition Acts passed in 1798 during John Adams' Administration in order to curb the political freedom of the (Jeffersonian) Democratic-Republican Party. It is worth observing, in the first place, that John Adams was a great American Revolutionist, and that he had been one of the committee of three which participated in the drafting of the Declaration of Independence. It is stirring to know that it was in large part the resistance to these restraining acts which helped elect Jefferson President in 1800. But, while it is true that under Jefferson the Alien and Sedition Acts were permitted to lapse as the abominations they were, it is also true that Jefferson, himself, was sorely troubled by the insistent and unprincipled attacks upon him emanating from the Federalist press. The nature of these attacks may be indicated when it is stated that they were more vicious and indecent than the assaults of the Hearst press upon the New Deal. But what is not sufficiently known, and what is rarely quoted, is the fact that Jefferson, therefore, seriously urged the use of the principle of government intervention to prevent these kinds of written attacks. Thus, in 1803, Jefferson wrote to his friend, Governor McKean of Pennsylvania, as follows:

"The federalists, having failed in destroying the freedom of the press by their gag-law, seem to have attacked it in an opposite direction; that is by pushing its licentiousness and its

lying to such a degree of prostitution as to
deprive it of all credit. . . . This is a dangerous
state of things, and the press ought to be re-
stored to its credibility if possible. The restraints
provided by the laws of the States are sufficient
for this, if applied. And I have, therefore, long
thought that a few prosecutions of the most
prominent offenders would have a wholesome
effect in restoring the integrity of the presses.
Not a general prosecution, for that would look
like persecution; but a selected one."

While seeking to indicate the substantial and
real nature of the struggle for human freedom,
it is pertinent to note that during the Great
French Revolution, in 1791, one decree outlawed trade unions as "an attack upon liberty
and upon the Declaration of the Rights of Man,"
while another made advocacy of a monarchy
punishable by execution. Thus, did the revolutionary bourgeoisie deal a blow at each of its
foes, the workers and the nobility.

John Stuart Mill

Much of the same considerations apply to
the powerful writings of John Stuart Mill, especially his *On Liberty, Considerations on Repre-*
sentative Government, and in his most rigorous
work, clearly indicating the advance over Jefferson, *The Subjection of Women.* These are, of
course, classical arguments for democratic rights,
embodied in the immortal and much quoted
line: "truth has no chance but in proportion
as every side of it, every opinion which embodies
any fraction of the truth, not only find ad-

vocates, but is so advocated as to be listened to."

But again, placed in his time and place—mid-19th-century England — and his class — upper middle-class, his father an official for the East India Company—one is prepared for the rather severe limitations that Mill, in fact, put around his concepts of liberty and representative government. He wrote in the midst of intensified political agitation, by the industrial bourgeoisie and the working class, for the enlargement of their democratic rights, and so the questions with which he dealt had a particular relationship to specific burning issues. The special problem of the time, as Gladstone remarked somewhat later, was to "get the working class within the pale of the constitution," i.e., work them in toward participation in political sovereignty without their transforming the basic status quo.

Mill opposed the secret ballot; he opposed paying Members of Parliament (for only the well-to-do and those of independent means are masters of their own minds) ; he wanted only taxpayers to vote; an educational test for voting; all recipients of public aid barred from the vote; those in "higher" occupations to have a greater number of votes, so that the employer, for example, would have a more numerous suffrage than the worker. Mill favored the limitation of freedom of speech, in terms of what Holmes later called the "clear and present danger," and the examples Mill himself gave demonstrate that the danger that worried him was the danger to private property. Mill was an elitist, expressing contempt for the "collective mediocrity" of the people generally, and tribute to the decisive influence of the "gifted One or Few."

Mill was a colonialist, a rather backward one, in fact, even for his time, and his Anglo-Saxon chauvinism is painful to read. He detested "the American institution" alleging men's equality.

These are some of the fairly severe limitations of John Stuart Mill, but despite them all, he does produce works which, placed in their context, argue forcefully and persuasively for an expansion of existent freedoms—in England, at that time, for certain of its inhabitants—much of the logic of which, as with Milton and Jefferson, has applications transcending their time and their origin.

Significant in examining the matter of freedom in history, freedom as process, is the actuality of advances in human freedom. Where social transformations achieve such advances, the movement accomplishing them will also consolidate them, or try to, and normally not allow them to be questioned or, at least, seriously challenged.

Thus, the destruction of monarchy is of the essence of the French Revolution, and it is not a subject for refutation, so far as the accomplishment of that Revolution is concerned. So, too, our Constitution "guarantees" to each state a Republican form of government and this fundamental result of our Revolution likewise is not subject to refutation. So, too, the Thirteenth Amendment to our Constitution, bought with so much blood, is supposed to settle, once for all, the question of the existence of chattel slavery; it settles it by forbidding that institution, the same institution which shortly before the Amendment represented four-billion-dollars-worth of private property, and the ownership of which was the most precious "right" of 350,000 slaveowners, who, on the basis of that "right," had dominated the Government. The question of chattel slavery, then, is settled, so far as this Republic is concerned, at this stage of its development.

So, too, at Potsdam, it was agreed that the German people were free to form any parties, any organizations they wished, and to publish and argue for any views they desired, *except fascist,* for fascism, in all forms and guises and organizational institutions, was to be extirpated, and this, too, according to the Treaty, was not to be a matter for future negotiation.

In this connection there is a perceptive passage in Mill's *Liberty* which is quoted very rarely, perhaps because it does not argue for abstracting human freedom. Mill wrote:

"As mankind improves, the number of doctrines which are no longer disputed or doubted will be constantly on the increase; and the well-being of mankind may almost be measured by the number and gravity of the truths which have reached the point of being uncontested. The cessation, on one question after another, of serious controversy, is one of the necessary incidents of the consolidation of opinion; a consolidation as salutary in the case of true opinions, as it is dangerous and noxious when the opinions are erroneous. But though this gradual narrowing of the bounds of diversity of opinion is necessary in both senses of the term, being at once inevitable and indispensable, we are not therefore obliged to conclude that all its consequences will be beneficial."

We have seen, in the cases of Milton, Jefferson and Mill, how decisive were class considerations in their own definitions of freedom. It may be added that hitherto, government and writings about government have been matters for "gentlemen" only; this has meant the *assumption* that others than "gentlemen" were objects of government and nothing more.*

Historically, it is a fact that in class-exploitative societies, People—often spelled with an upper-case "P"—were those of property, while the people, or, the inhabitants, the masses, the general population, were all other human beings domiciled in the area but more or less deprived of all rights and certainly of participation in the exercise of political power. Just as today when one writes of the doings of Society, with an uppercase "S," he has in mind the thin layer riding atop society and battening on it, so has there been heretofore in class societies a similar distinction between people and People.

This is fundamental to Mill's own limitations on liberty. This is why he repeatedly excludes from his category of people fit for freedom, those he calls "rude," or lacking "instruction" or divorced from "rational" capacities. (Incidentally,

---

*Of Mill, Edmund Leach aptly writes: "His concern was with the freedom of English gentlemen, not the freedom of humanity at large." This is in his "Law as Condition of Freedom," in David Bidney, ed., *The Concept of Freedom in Anthropology* (The Hague, 1963), p. 75.

in one place, he offers as an example of such incapacitated people the Russian peasant!) It is fundamental to the whole conception held by exploiters as to the "poor"—poor both in terms of being without wealth and also without capacities, and therefore without wealth. It is organically related to the racist concept, which, given enough stimulation by capitalism's greed, soon rationalizes the actual sub-humanity of the victims!

This is why Swift, in his *Thoughts on Various Subjects,* held it to be axiomatic that "law in a free country is, or ought to be, the determination of the majority of those who have property in land," and Defoe, writing on *The Original Power of the Collective Body of the People of England,* made clear that the possessors of property were "the proper owners of the country" and that other inhabitants were "but sojourners, like lodgers in a house." Voltaire, whose very name rings of the French Revolution, and is synonymous with the Age of Reason, wrote in 1768: "As regards the people, they will always be stupid and barbarous. They are oxen which require a yoke, a goad, and some hay." Thus Voltaire, not Louis XIV! And obviously, here there are important distinctions between the people—oxen—and People, such as Voltaire.

This conception of the brutishness of the masses is important in explaining why many reject socialism as impossible because of "human nature." It is basic to the thinking of Robert Michels in his extremely influential volume *Political Parties: A Sociological Study of the Oligarchical Tendencies of Modern Democracy,* first published in 1915.* Here the theme is that "democracy is inconceivable without organization" and organization is impossible without oligarchy; hence, democracy is not realizable. Not sufficiently noticed in this work, is one of its fundamental postulates: "The incompetence of the masses is almost universal throughout the domains of political life, and this constitutes the most solid foundation of the power of the leaders."

This is at the heart of all kinds of elitist thinking, so potent in the "New Conservatism" —for example, in the books of Walter Lippmann during the 1950's. It has reached the point where a young American scholar, E. Digby Baltzell, begins his useful examination of the realities of ruling class power in the United States, selecting one city as a case study, *Philadelphia Gentlemen: The Making of a National Upper Class* (The Free Press, 1958), with the sentence: "Granted, all complex societies—aristocratic, democratic, or totalitarian—are oligarchical in that the few rule the many."

Michels' postulate is false. There is not mass incompetence; there is mass deprivation and oppression and exploitation. The deprivation brings with it degrees of incompetence in necessary skills, but the lack is never so decisive as upper-class ideologists think. And this is not a vicious circle, with neither end nor beginning, for the exploitation comes first and reared upon

*Within the past ten years, this book has been made available in two paperback editions, Collier and Dover; and in two clothbound editions, Free Press and Peter Smith.

this comes whatever incompetence there may be. Eliminating the exploitation *makes possible* the removal of the last remnants of such incompetence.

Democracy and Class

The bourgeoisie wants politics to be confined to struggles among varied propertied groups, not between the propertied and the propertyless. A mirror of this desire is the Constitution of the United States, wherein, among other things, is the aim to obscure fundamental class antagonism and to give the appearance of the government as a balance wheel—impartial, accurate, and just. At the same time that the political grants made to the people as a whole serve as important mediums for struggle, they also serve to deflect the target of the struggle into channels picked by the political representatives of the propertied groups.

The bourgeois revolutionaries sense that *real* democracy requires a substantial identity of interest; requires an end to classes. They see that then will come basic unanimity. Madison, for example, writing to Jefferson in 1787, said that if one had a society whose members had common interests then "the decisions could only turn on mere opinion concerning the good of the whole," and where the society was basically homogeneous, without "a distinction of property," there "a pure republic" or "a simple democracy" would be possible. But he found this then, with good historical reasons, illusory and so he saw the task as one of protecting the inequality while maintaining the republican form, i.e., he saw the solution as bourgeois-democracy.

In the Constitutional Convention, Madison put the matter very clearly:

"In framing a system which we wish to last for ages, we should not lose sight of the changes which ages will produce. An increase of population will of necessity increase the proportion of those who will labor under all the hardships of life, and secretly sigh for a more equal distribution of its blessings. These may in time outnumber those who are placed above the feelings of indigence. According to the equal laws of suffrage, the power will slide into the hands of the former. No agrarian attempts have yet been made in this country, but symptoms, of a leveling spirit, as we have understood, have sufficiently appeared in certain quarters to give notice of the future danger."

Madison, returning to this question of questions in the 1830's, confessed that its solution was beyond him: how to have popular sovereignty and retain an economic system in which a few possessed the means of production. Great alterations in government would be necessary, he was sure, as population mounted—he thought the 1930's would be a turning point—and, "To the effect of these changes, intellectual, moral, and social, the institutions and laws of the country must be adapted, and it will require for the task all the wisdom of the wisest patriots."

The turning point suggested by Madison has come and gone, and with it much of the world has indeed changed; and the rest is in the process of those changes. They have indeed required and will continue to require all the wisdom, and courage, of which mankind is capable. But the new dawn is here, and with its rise a new definition of "the people" is on the agenda. In our era that definition is infinitely wider, very much more democratic, than was true when Milton or Voltaire or Jefferson or Madison or Mill wrote.

We close this brief inquiry into some facets of the complex history of human freedom with a quotation concerning not socialism in the abstract, but socialism as it has been built in one of the largest states on earth. The quotation comes from a non-Communist—for in the given circumstances, such a source may be more persuasive. Dealing with the Soviet Union, Harold J. Laski, the late leader of the British Labour Party, in one of his last volumes, *Liberty in the Modern State* (N.Y., 1949), wrote:

"It has been part of the strategy of the enemies of freedom in part to decry the accomplishment of the Soviet Union's makers, and in part to declare that the price is too heavy for the end. It is vital for those who care for freedom to maintain a proper perspective in this matter. The Soviet Union has been the pioneer of a new civilization. The conditions upon which it began the task of its building were of a magnitude unexampled in our experience. Its leaders came to power in a country accustomed only to bloody tyranny, racked and impoverished by unsuccessful war. Its peoples were overwhelmingly illiterate and untrained in the use of that industrial technology upon which the standards of modern civilization depend. Its task of construction was begun amidst civil war, intervention from without, famine and pestilence. For the first years of the regime's existence the people lived quite literally in a state of siege. . . . No doubt Lenin and his colleagues were responsible, in the first seven years of the Revolution, for blunders, mistakes, even crimes. It is nevertheless true that, in those years, they accomplished a remarkable work of renovation. They accomplished it, moreover, in such a fashion that, within ten years of the overthrow of the Czar, they were able to proceed to the socialization of the productive system.

"In the last decade, the achievements have been immense. The war has been won, unemployment has been abolished; illiteracy has been conquered; the growing productivity of the Soviet Union stands in startling contrast to the deliberate organization of scarcity in the capitalist states. In the treatment of criminals, in the scientific handling of backward peoples, in the application of science to industry and agriculture, in the conquest of racial prejudice, and in the provision of opportunity to the individual—in the full sense the career opened to the talents—the Soviet Union stands today in the forefront of civilization. It is, of course, true that, judged by the standards of Great Britain and the United States, its material levels of life are low; it has not rivalled in twenty years the unimpeded century-long development of the most progressive capitalist states. The true comparison, of course, is with pre-revolutionary

Russia; and the gains, both material and spiritual, are immense. In wages, hours of labor, conditions of sanitation and safety, industrial security, and educational opportunity, the comparison is at every point favorable to the new regime."

The two decades that have followed these words from Laski have tended, I think, to confirm their validity. After 50 years, the Bolshevik Revolution and the State it forged stand as a central event and force for social justice, human equality, and peace.

This overall judgement is rendered with full awareness of the aberrations, mistakes and crimes committed in the name of "socialism" during those five decades. These failings derived out of the heritages of the past—especially in Russia—and out of the extraordinarily difficult circumstances under which the transformation was carried out. All this, plus the horrors of war and the contest with fascism—and the personal, subjective and psychological inadequacies and vices—produced veritable atrocities that slandered the concept of Marxism.

These did not, however, overbalance the total reckoning of the socialist revolution; their existence was contrary to the needs of that revolution; they were finally exposed and condemned by the revolutionists themselves.

All in all, the remarkable economic, technical, educational, health and cultural accomplishments of socialism, its decisive contribution to the defeat of fascism, its effective opposition to racism and colonialism, and its indispensable support of the struggle for peace, make the record of socialism the best hope of mankind.

2. On the Nature of Freedom

We move now from considering freedom in history, as process, to an examination of the nature of freedom itself.

The State and Political Power

The question of the state and the nature of political power, may be chosen as a starting point for our inquiry, for certainly the presence and the nature of freedom have hinged upon both, to a great degree.

On the whole, in classical political theory—from Aristotle to Locke to Burke—the state, or government, is viewed as a vehicle for the preservation of the existing societal status quo. In this literature, fundamental to that status quo was the property relationship characterizing it and, in a decisive fashion, determining it. From this analysis was derived the axiom that government existed in order to protect private property. That this should be axiomatic was perfectly natural, since all hitherto existing states had been built upon the private ownership and control of the means of production, with differences in such societies reflecting differences in the kinds of productive means so owned, and the relations of production arising therefrom, but not in the fact of their private ownership.

Connected with this was the idea that the

existence of private property was the prerequisite of civilization. No doubt, this idea was tied to the fact that it was on the basis of the division of labor consequent upon such possession of property in the means of production that technological and productive advances became possible upon which were erected the accoutrements of civilization. Therefore—and the transition appears altogether logical—it is only those who are among the propertied who should be among those who govern. Clearly, if private property is the basis of civilization, and if government exists to protect that private property and thereby maintain civilization, then surely those possessed of that private property are those in whom and only in whom is properly vested governmental authority. Or, as the first Chief Justice of the United States Supreme Court, John Jay, put it: "Those who own the country, should govern it."

This idea seemed all the more reasonable as it became more and more clear, to those benefiting from and fostering the idea, that just as the security of private property was of the essence of civilization, so only those who possessed private property were really civilized. It was but a step from this comforting observation, to the clinching conception that those who possessed private property not only were the civilized and therefore should be the government—whose main purpose, remember, was the security of that property—but that they were also the ones alone *capable* of conducting government. And that they *were* capable was proven, so went the argument, by the very fact that they had succeeded in acquiring private property. Hence, to cite again the words of a well-known American, it was, as John Adams said, "the rich, the well-born and the able" who manifestly should be in charge of government. What is to be noted in particular in this quotation, is John Adams' assumption that what he was offering was a string of synonyms, and that, *of course*, the rich were the well-born, and that, *of course*, the rich and the well-born were the able.

From this the corollary was clear, and was made explicit in the classical literature, that while the rich were rich because they were able, and that being rich gave them opportunities to enhance further notable abilities, the poor on the other hand, were poor because they were not able and that, therefore, their surroundings were such as to intensify their inherent inadequacy.

In all this it was assumed, as was natural for rulers of societies based upon the private ownership of the means of production, that acquisitiveness was of the essence of "human nature," and that the more successfully acquisitive one was the more notably "human" was he. That is, the very word "success" connoted wealth; a "successful" man was one who had accumulated a goodly property. Happy it was, too, that the accumulation of property demonstrated the existence of superior ability; hence, the wealth was a just reward for such ability as it was, simultaneously, the proof of that ability.

Note that, in a sense, the existence of the state was the existence of a necessary evil; that is, the requirement of a state demonstrated the evil inherent in mankind, an evil which reflected itself particularly in unlawful rapacity for the possessions of another, whether that be his wife or some less animated property. Note, too, that it was the poor who, being no good at all, and therefore poor, were especially prone to this rapacity, for obvious reasons. Hence, it was the duty of the rich, in the name of civilization, itself, to restrain the poor. That is to say, it was required of the rich—who, being rich were relatively less evil than the poor and therefore thrice blessed with worldly goods—to restrain the poor and to govern them. Such restraint was the main function of government in general.

Sovereignty, then, or political power, inhered in the owners, with the classical forms for such sovereignty being either the tyrant or the oligarch; or, for small areas with homogeneous populations, a so-called democracy. With the concentration upon land ownership and the tying of control over productive labor to such ownership, which characterized the pre-capitalist era, more and more the idea developed that ownership of the earth inhered in God who had designated earthly rulers in clearly defined hierarchical patterns, and that these divinely-anointed ones held their property in accordance with His will. At the apex was the one earthly figure, in varying geographical areas, who was The Sovereign; it was in him personally that the sovereignty of the political entity resided.

Hence, sovereign always was spelled with a capital S; his person was adorned with symbols of supreme power and dignity; and his name was gilded with phrases like His Supreme High-

ness, His Majesty, His Eminence, His Most
Worshipful Person, The Sun God, The Supreme
Ruler, and other monuments to man's verbal
ingenuity when properly impelled and sufficiently rewarded.

The capitalist revolution against feudalism
represented a two-pronged attacked upon this
ancient and medieval view of sovereignty. In
the first place, capitalism's destruction of feudalism carried with it the creation of the modern
nation, and the complex feeling known as
nationalism. In the second place, capitalism's
destruction of feudalism required justification
for an attack upon ancient and sanctified forms
of rule, and also required the participation of
masses of people of small or of no property in
order to overcome the power of the aristocracy
and the landlords.

The first development, the appearance of the
modern reality of nation and idea of nationalism, meant that the sovereignty became national
rather than personal. That is, for example,
France existed in French men and French
women; they make up France, they *are* France.
Which is another way of saying that France is
not that which is reached and dominated by
the sword of Louis XIV, which had been the
meaning of Louis' insistence: "The State, I am
the State." Louis there was denouncing the new-
fangled concept of nationality, that France is
not Louis but is the French people.

This tendency to repudiate the personal quality of sovereignty was reinforced by the tactical
and political needs of the bourgeoisie in leading
the revolution against feudalism. That class

itself had to justify its own demands for sovereignty, and in this direct way tended to make its character plural; at the same time, requiring mass assistance, such aid was justified and obtained on the basis of mass participation in sovereignty. True, from the earliest times, this bourgeoisie, even when revolutionary, was sorely troubled as to how far the masses might go; how seriously they might take the idea of sharing in actual sovereignty; and how difficult would be the matter of controlling them with their vast numbers, once the feudal system was destroyed. This fear permeated the revolutions in Europe during the 17th and 18th centuries; it was present in our own American Revolution. This is the meaning of Gouverneur Morris' warning, in 1774, that he feared where the revolutionary stirrings might end. "For the masses," said Morris, "this is a red dawning and mefears that ere noon, they will bite." Morris meant that they would bite not only the British overlords, which would be all right, but that they would bite the propertied in America, too, and that was not all right.

From this anti-feudal revolution developed the modern concept of popular sovereignty, really a verbal paradox, reflecting a political revolution undoing centuries of tradition and practice where the sovereign was divine and individual, and where the point of his sovereignty was that he ruled *over* the populace. Now with the anti-feudal revolution, came forward the idea not of sovereignty as being personal and being displayed in its domination over the people, but of sovereignty as being multiple and consisting, properly, in rule by, for, and on behalf of the people.

True it is that this revolution was not one that challenged the private ownership of the means of production. It was not one, therefore, which challenged the basic idea of the function of the state—to protect such property relationships. Hence there persisted, in this first propounding of the concept of rule by the people, a limiting feature in the definition of who constituted the people. The people were those with property; for clearly, still, the purpose of government was the protection of property. Hence, that meant protection against the rapacity of those without property, uncivilized and incapable as they were. Hence, too, that meant that only those with property properly could participate in the exercise of governmental functions. Therefore, it was the propertied who were the people; the remainder of the population were inhabitants, residents, masses, but not people.

This posed an awful riddle for the theoreticians of the new order: The people are sovereign, most of them do not own the means of production, the purpose of the state is to protect such ownership; how, then, to prevent the majority from using their power to undo such ownership, and so transform the nature of the state? So brilliant a thinker as James Madison frankly confessed that he did not know how to solve this problem; he thought, as we have seen, it would come to a head in about the 1930's, and he expressed the wish that by then sufficient wisdom would exist to untie this knot!

Madison was remarkably astute; never did he more clearly demonstrate his genius than when he confessed his perplexity and announced his hope.

On the Theory of Political Parties

When sovereignty was personal, political parties, other than that representing the Crown, were held to be seditious and, therefore, manifestly not to be permitted. This was because of the nature of a political party, an organization of like-minded people seeking to gain state power in order to accomplish certain purposes held by them to be of great consequence. If, however, sovereignty, that is to say, state power, belonged to the Monarch, then clearly no group of people legally could work together for the purpose of acquiring such power for themselves or their party.

It is for this reason that in England, where the power of feudalism was broken first, the modern political party did not appear until the reign of George III, that is, until the middle of the 18th century. That, also, is why when a party in opposition to the Crown did appear there, it was labelled the Whig Party, a term of opprobrium, Whig meaning in old Scottish, "horsethief."

Such an opposition party, however, did appear in 18th century England, no matter what the extant political theory was and no matter how intense was the opposition to its appearance on the part of the Crown, because with the smashing of feudalism in England, the bourgeoisie insisted on making that victory safe by acquiring domination over the state apparatus. Hence, since in fact the modern political party resulted from and represented the existence of different classes with varying and often contradicting interests, the rise of a mercantile and industrial bourgeoisie in England meant that that class would insist on organizing politically with the purpose of taking state power away from the landed aristocracy and the Court circles.

Yet, given the theory of sovereignty inhering in the person of the King, and the whole structure of government in England corresponding to that theory, such a development obviously would encounter stiff ideological and organizational opposition.

What happened was that the objective social reality, the rise of the bourgeoisie, produced de facto opposition parties. The Court and the landholders sought to smash this development by charging that it was unprecedented and downright seditious. The bourgeoisie sought to manufacture precedents by reference to "rights of Englishmen" enunciated under quite different circumstances, and to overcome the charge of sedition by swearing their loyalty to the King's person, while seeking to alter the legal structure by enlarging the powers of Parliament.

The structural alteration was accomplished, helped along considerably by the success of the American Revolution, by the last years of George III's reign, and the modern parliamentary system, with its Prime Minister and Cabinet, date from that period. Ideological adjustment accompanied this social and legal change, and is

most prominently associated with the name of
Edmund Burke. It is Burke who developed most
cogently a rationalization for the existence of
multiple parties, though each party was supposed
to be seeking exclusive domination over state
power.

As we have indicated, this process took several
generations, and from the 16th through much of
the 18th centuries it was accompanied by fearful
instability in English governments and by much
violence. Most Prime Ministers of England in
this nearly two-hundred-year period were removed from office by trial and condemnation,
suffering either execution, long imprisonment,
or exile.

But, given the achievement of sufficient basic
change, Burke's ideological solution could both
be arrived at and approved. What Burke suggested was the co-existence of multiple parties,
on the basis of two common points of agreement, namely, loyalty to the private ownership
of the means of production and to the symbol
of the Crown.

In this way, the assumption continued that
government belonged to the propertied classes
and existed, fundamentally, for the purpose of
preserving that private property. Where gentlemen of property agreed on that, they could form
different political parties based upon the ownership of different forms and kinds of property,
but all such parties would agree on the two
fundamentals and thus would be loyal (and
legal) political parties. The differences among
parties, then, would reflect differences in outlook
and interest of varying kinds of propertied

classes; but these differences would be kept on the tactical level so far as the basic interests of the state and of civilization were concerned. They would be differences as to how best to advance the interests of the state and civilization, with both resting upon the private ownership of the means of production. Any political party or grouping which did not agree to these fundamentals would not be a bona fide political party, but would rather be a seditious organization.

The British, with their genius for institutionalizing things, institutionalized this solution, too. It appears in the existence of the ruling party, or The Government, and in the leading minority party, or Her Majesty's Most Loyal Opposition. Everything is capitalized and everything is proper. This reflects itself further in the fact that two Members of Parliament are paid by the state a higher salary than all other Members—one is the Prime Minister, who is paid extra for his services as Her Majesty's First Minister; the other is The Leader of Her Majesty's Loyal Opposition, who is paid for his duties as that Leader, and who is assumed to be performing necessary functions for the stability of Her Realm and of civilization by leading the (tactical) Opposition.

The American Experience

What is the original attitude toward political parties when success is achieved in establishing a republic based upon the sovereignty of the people? If political power is held, in fact, by the people, how in theory can several parties legitimately exist if the purpose of a political party is to obtain state power? The answer was that such parties could not legitimately exist; that was exactly the attitude of the Founding Fathers. It was held that the existence of political parties in England reflected the corruption and tyrannical character of that government against which the colonists had rebelled successfully. For if the people were in power, then a political party seeking power could only be counter-revolutionary, *i.e.*, could only seek to undo the sovereignty of the people.

On this same reasoning, the original theory of democracy was that it would exist on the basis not of diversity of opinion, but rather on the basis of unanimity of opinion. This unanimity would flow from the common interest of all and from the share of all in the exercise of political power. For this reason, too, it was assumed that the existence of political parties in a democratic republic would be anachronistic and/or illegal.

This is why there is no mention of political parties in the Constitution of the United States. This is why political parties as such were in poor repute in the 18th and early 19th centuries in the United States. This is why President Washington, in his last Message to Congress, warned against the appearance of "factions," a synonym then for parties, as threatening the very existence of the Republic. This is why, when Jefferson went about organizing his political opposition to Hamilton, and of course did it in the form of a political party, he did this secretly and bound his friends, like James Madison, to the keeping of that secrecy. This is why one does not find the open acknowledgment of the existence of political parties as such in the United States until 1816, when the first explicitly labelled national convention of a political party was held—and that was the Hartford Convention which marked the demise of the Federalist Party.

Related to the concept of unanimity, so far as the political base of the new republic was concerned, was the provision in the Constitution guaranteeing to each State a republican form of government. For the Founders, a government based upon the sovereignty of the people had to be republican in form. But in the guarantee of such a form we have a paradox. The paradox is that the same document which asserts the sovereignty of the people simultaneously insists that the form of government for each of the States *must* be republican—that is, here is a provision prohibiting the sovereign people, who, being sovereign, presumably are omnipotent, from destroying the Republic. This means that the people, while sovereign, are saying, under the Constitution, that they may not have any form of government other than republican, which is to say, they are forbidden to have a monarchy, the alternative closest at hand and the form just recently revolutionized. Monarchy was a form, let it be noted, that might very well have come into being in America, for the English Crown had not given up, at that time, its hope of undoing the American Revolution; nor were there missing from American life Tories and monarchists, some of them, indeed, in high military and political circles.

This prohibition is quite absolute; it holds no matter how large a number of people in any particular State might want something else. If, for instance, 95 per cent of the people of New York State should desire that Mr. Rockefeller be their King, and if they proceeded to install the aforesaid gentleman as King Nelson, the United States would be required by the Constitution to forbid this course, even if that entailed the use of force against the overwhelming majority of presumably deluded New Yorkers.

While this sounds absurd today, since the restoration of monarchy in the United States is not a danger, the theory behind it exists and remains valid. Thus, for instance, it forms the heart of the Potsdam Treaty terminating World War II; there, the Allies pledged that the German people were to have a free form of government, and that they could choose any form of government they wished, except fascist. That is, if 90 per cent of the German people wanted a fascist form of government, they were not to be free to choose one. This prohibition was made in the name of advancing freedom; the prohibition does advance freedom, and it is the failure to enforce that prohibition which has damaged the cause of human freedom.

Size and Homogeneity

There remain two particular features of the American experience at the Republic's founding that are especially relevant to a consideration of the nature of freedom. Both involved the question of the feasibility and the durability of republican-democratic government and both had appeared constantly in the classical literature on political science. These were the insistence, in the first place, that such government was possible only within a small geographical area and among a homogeneous population; and, in the second place, that even where such territorial and demographic requirements were met, such government would not last long because of an allegedly immutable tendency toward the concentration of power in the hands of smaller and smaller groups of men, until the democratic-republican form of government had been transformed into an oligarchy and a tyranny—whereupon, possibly, went the classical literature, the whole cycle might start revolving again.

The Revolutionary Fathers of the American Republic were aware, of course, of these arguments; and those among them who ardently desired the preservation of the democratic-republican form worked out an answer to both, the two parts of which were as inter-related as were the two difficulties. In both, Thomas Jefferson and James Madison were especially prominent.

Quite boldly, it was argued that far from vast size being an impassable barrier to the erection of a viable republican form of government, the enormous size of the infant republic would be a source of strength and would help make it possible for the infant to reach adulthood. The theory was that while pure and direct democracy obviously would require, given limitations on travel and communication, very confined political entities, on the style of the ancient Greek city-states, this would not be true for a republican-democracy, where indirection through the method of representation would replace direct democratic government.

For that type of government, great expanse would be an advantage, in terms of durability, for—especially in the United States, where the great size was accompanied by marked sectional and regional differences—it would make impossible the concentration of power in one particular area to such a degree as to outweigh the strength of the other areas. And just as the very size would make unwholesome concentration of political power most difficult, so the great variation in the nature of the numerous sections also would make such concentration quite unlikely.

The two features combined, then, would seem to make reasonably certain the impossibility of such a concentration of power in any one geographical area as to threaten the existence of the democratic-republican form. The political structure which would reflect and express the advantages flowing from the great size and the marked sectional divergencies would be the federal one, with the multiple form of sovereignty existing in the sovereignty of each of the States and the sovereignty of the central government in matters concerning the whole nation, as such.

The defense against unwholesome concentration of power which geography offered would be enhanced by the fact that there was a widespread dispersion of different and often antagonistic, or at least rivaling, economic classes—as

planters, small farmers, merchants, financiers, industrialists, fur-traders, fishermen, etc.—whose diversity would militate against social concentration of power, just as geography militated against
area concentration. This would be strengthened
further by the diversity of national origins and
religious backgrounds of the people making up
the American nationality, which, again, from the
demographic viewpoint, would reinforce the tendency toward the dispersal of political power
already present geographically and economically.

Notice that nothing in the above considerations contradicted the fundamental assumption
of political theory, namely, that governments
existed for the purpose of preserving private
property and that, therefore, the governors were
the propertied and the governed were the propertyless. The problem of tyranny was the problem of the concentration of power in the hands
of one element among the propertied and the
use of such power to violate the interests of
other propertied groups; against this, the democratic republic would assure some protection.
The problem of anarchy was represented by the
seizure of power by the non-propertied. This was
anarchic in that it violated the classically postu-
lated purposes of government; government so
transformed became non-government. That is to
say, it became anarchy, and against that all men
of property, no matter of what kind—i.e., all men
of respectability and of good sense—would be
united.

The Revolutionary Fathers felt that these federal arrangements would be helpful, too, in
counteracting the allegedly inherent tendency

of democratic republican governments toward greater and greater concentration of political power into fewer and fewer hands until oligarchy appeared. But there was another device which they felt also would help in preventing that concentration of power which hitherto had doomed all attempts at democratic rule. And the Fathers believed that this might work despite their own acute awareness of the attractions that power held for those of mortal flesh, an awareness that they frequently expressed in language too long neglected by the 20th century.

This device was the system of checks and balances and the separation of powers which were made fundamental features of the constitutional structure of the United States. It was thought that making each of the three elements of government—executive, legislative, judicial—independent of each other and co-equal in power would serve to prevent the concentration of power into the hands of one clique or one man, and the man especially feared in the light of 18th-century experience was the executive. In addition to this separation, there was the system of checks and balances manifested in the two-house legislature with the concurrence of each necessary for the passage of a law, and then the need of executive approval, or, if vetoed, the overcoming of this veto requiring a two-thirds vote. Such arrangements, it was felt, made the appearance of tyranny, especially in the guise then best known, i.e., monarchy, as nearly impossible as human ingenuity could devise.

Once again, the Fathers had in mind not only the prevention of tyranny, as they understood it, but also of anarchy, as they understood, and feared, that. Hence, both the federal structure and the system of checks and balances made very difficult the effective exercise of real political power by the masses of the people who did not possess the means of production. But exactly this, too, was a goal if democratic-republican government were to endure, for the first object of government as such—all government, no matter what its form—was the protection of the private possession of the means of production, a basic arrangement characterizing most hitherto existing forms of civilization.

It is worth noting that this latter purpose has been expressed often in the literature; however, the former purpose, the prevention of tyranny, has been less fully comprehended and less often noticed. The two elements were present together, however, as was natural for property owners who had just led a national and anticolonial revolution, which, with great mass support and participation, had defeated the British throne.

As the maturing of capitalism into monopoly capitalism and imperialism makes more and more anachronistic and inhibiting the private ownership of the means of production—given the increasing socialization of the method of production, and the mounting objections of the colonial peoples—the assumption of rule by and for the propertied, in the face of the theory of popular sovereignty, becomes more and more impossible to reconcile. James Madison, therefore, projected that capitalism would be able to last, in its bourgeois-democratic form, until the mid-thirties of the twentieth century; then, predicted the Father of the U.S. Constitution, it would face a crisis of unprecedented and probably insoluble dimensions.

Implicit in the system of checks and balances is the concept of the benign nature of the government itself, meaning the particular, new, government set up as a result of the successful revolution in the New World. This represented an important break with the traditional idea of government being necessitated because of the villainy of mankind, and that therefore all government, in its origin, was attainted. Actually, the break was not complete, in the sense that this new government was still held to be—assumed to be, in fact—a government of and by the propertied for their protection; and the protection was needed because of the villainy of men, especially men without property. Still, there was present, in the roots of the U.S. government, this idea of its being benign.

Hence, given the system of checks and balances, the government itself is pictured as an impartial and paternal judge. This classless attitude toward the government, which has been and is so marked a characteristic of American popular opinion—among white Americans, at any rate— owes much of its viability to the manner in which this government was created. It was, in fact, the product of a popular revolution; and its present form was the result of reasoned debate among very able and patriotic gentlemen. It was, in fact, to a large degree, the product of popular agreement (or, at least, acquiescence); and it was, when thus established, the most advanced and most democratic government in existence. It maintained, with good objective reason, this reputation for some generations, with the only major blotch on that reputation being the existence of chattel slavery. But then, since the slaves were Negroes, the concept of racism was both necessary and handy for the retention of the view of the government as being really popular and really devoted, impartially, to the welfare of all its citizens.

Particularly significant was the manner in which the form of the U.S. government was created; that is, through debate and plebiscite. This seemed to confirm the New World republic as the living embodiment of the Age of Reason. And, since it was held that the destruction of feudalism ushered in a socio-economic system that really corresponded to the requirements of nature, that really was not artificial at all,* it seemed especially fitting that the infant revolutionary republic should deliberately go about creating a governmental structure that also reflected the triumph of reason over superstition, and therefore, of freedom over tyranny.

---

*In Marx's words, "the eternal Nature-ordained necessity for capitalist production," *Capital* (International Publishers, N. Y., 1967), Vol. I, p. 447.

3. Bourgeois Concepts of Freedom

Let us inquire into the meaning of freedom as conveyed in the literature on the subject produced in the course of the replacement of feudalism by capitalism and in the generations which have seen the growth and maturing of capitalism.

Freedom as Absence of Restraint

First, it is of the greatest importance to see that when capitalism replaced feudalism, advocates of the change and adherents of the new system insisted that both represented the triumph of reason and, hence, of freedom. Capitalism—that is to say, the free market, the system of free enterprise, the contractual agreement freely entered into by co-equal participants, the supremacy and immutability of the law of supply and demand, the nice manner in which the allegedly innate desire for personal aggrandizement fitted in with the accomplishment of human progress, the guarantee in all this that merit would be rewarded and lack of it penalized—this system, capitalism, it was held, was not really a social system in the sense of any kind of man-made construct but was rather the achievement in human relations of the reasonable and natural order of things. The law of supply and demand was as constant and as natural as the law of gravity; the whole functioning of free enterprise and unencumbered market was as inexorable and as natural as the coming and going of the tides.

The Age of Faith marks the era of feudalism; the Age of Reason marks the era of capitalism. This reason, which was the hallmark of the new science—itself the instrumentality for the development of that technique so consequential to the rise and appearance of capitalism and to its defeat of feudalism—was held to have triumphed not only in matters of physics and astronomy, but also in matters of politics and economics.

All this was enhanced by the fact that capitalism was in rebellion against the status-concentrating, closed, regulatory feudalism; what it sought was elimination of all artificial regulation and the free play of the newly discovered laws of politics and economics. Hence, *laissez-faire*—leave things alone, now that we have things arranged in their natural way.

The first component, then, of the concept of freedom in the classical bourgeois outlook is to see freedom as the absence of restraint. Freedom is viewed negatively; I do not mean by this, of course, that it is demeaned. On the contrary, it is highly valued. I mean only that freedom is viewed in terms of what government may not do; it is viewed in terms of opposition to power and to the exercise of power. Thus, Lord Morley, one of the keenest analysts of the problem of freedom among those operating outside the Marxist view, in a work revised by himself as late as 1921, emphasized that "liberty is not a positive force," and spoke of "liberty, or the absence of coercion," showing clearly that he felt the two ideas to be synonymous.*

Thus, while freedom is held to mean the absence of restraint, this absence applies to the citizens of the government; it is they who are free to the extent that they enjoy an absence of restraint. This carried with it a corollary, namely, the necessity to restrain the government, to delimit its power. So, the absence of governmental tyranny derives out of a restrained government. And, at times, the existence of such restraint is held to be synonymous with a free society, or with the existence of liberty. Thus, Dean Acheson, the former Secretary of State, writing in *The Yale Review* (Summer, 1959), declares that "the rights of Englishmen . . . were specific and detailed restraints upon power" —a rather paradoxical posing of rights as deriving from restraints, but again emphasizing the negative quality of the rights, or the negative quality of freedom. Hence it is that in the classical enunciation of freedoms, the Bill of Rights in the U.S. Constitution, one finds that these rights are actually an enumeration of those things which the government is forbidden to do.

The concentration on this assumes the evil nature of power; it assumes that the foe of freedom is power. This is not a far-fetched assumption when one remembers the historical

*John Viscount Morley, *On Compromise* (Thinker's Library, 1933, 3rd impression, London, 1946), p. 125. In a footnote at this point Morley stated that "there is a sense" "in which liberty is a positive force"; but he went on to write that it is so in that it has "a bracing influence on character."

record as to the uses of power. But the fact that it is an assumption and is so deeply ingrained in one's thinking, sometimes makes it an item that we do not really think about. Note, however, again, the assumption of the evil quality of political power; from this follows the axiom that to the extent such power is curbed to that extent is freedom present; *i.e.*, to that extent is there an absence of restraint upon the person.

These postulates work and are meant to work only if a fundamental proposition is adhered to. That fundamental proposition, we repeat, is that the basic ingredient of civilization is the private ownership of the means of production, for the protection of which the government and the state exist. The whole point of the superiority of capitalism is that it provides a system, allegedly, for the natural and unencumbered functioning of private-property ownership. Hence, since that system has been discovered—a truth found, like gravity—the less government, the better. Indeed, with such a system, government itself is but a necessary evil.

It is necessary because the poor we always have with us; these are the incapable ones, those without ability, without merit; hence these are the poor and they are without ownership of the means of production; and for them, government is necessary. It is necessary to see to it that they do not, in their ignorance, avarice, and sinfulness, destroy the social order, destroy civilization. It is needed, also, to see that no one element or group among the propertied so far forget themselves as to seek to usurp all power for themselves in order to en-

rich themselves at the expense of others owning property. With this arrangement, the government will prevent both tyranny and anarchy;
a just government will prevail holding even the
balance wheels of a natural political economy,
marked by reason and blessed by God.

Freedom Purely Political

In addition to the ideas of the restraint of
power and the absence of restraint upon citizens,
very important to the classical bourgeois concept of freedom was its limitation to matters
of politics. That is, classically, freedom is purely
political; it has no relevance to the economic.
This follows as a matter of course if one accepts
the view that capitalism *is* economic freedom;
that capitalism is the achievement of reason in
matters of economy. Accepting this view makes
mischievous at best and tyrannical at worst any
meddling with, any regulating of, the economy.

This view had in the 17th and 18th centuries
less inconsistencies than it appears to have today,
at least to many people, because in those centuries the fact that government's first obligation
was the security of private property was institutionalized in that only the propertied were
allowed to participate in selecting those who
did the governing, and only the highly propertied were allowed themselves to be among
the governors.

Nevertheless, the potency of this idea remains
great even in so developed a bourgeois-democratic republic as the United States. Thus, it
is still generally assumed that one's own busi-

ness really is his own; again, there remains a quite grudging acceptance of any kind of regulatory enactment, whether for the safety of the workers or the purity (or, at least, harmlessness) of the product issuing from the business. And the whole process of labor relations is still held to be fundamentally outside the ken of government, with government intervening only when matters of public security become involved, or when it appears as an "impartial" arbiter or arranger. The impact of the idea is reflected, also, in the persistency with which matters of health and social welfare were confined to the mercies of private medicine or "charity."

Here a remark by Marx is especially apt: "What could better show the character of the capitalist mode of production," he asked,* "than the necessity that exists for forcing upon it, by Acts of Parliament, the simplest appliances for maintaining cleanliness and health?"

Marx properly emphasizes not only the revealing quality of this necessity; he emphasizes also the fact that struggle is required to obtain acquiescence in the establishment of such elementary decencies.

That the classical ideas of *laissez faire* are changing, and that concepts of a "welfare state," of social legislation, of Keynesism are more and more common, reflect the inadequacies of capitalism, its instability, and the rising challenges to it—both within and without, in the developments and advances registered in socialist societies.

Even so, without preparations for and the

* Marx, *Capital* (cited edition), I, p. 481.

actual conducting of wars, it appears unlikely
that capitalism would have achieved the tenuous
and choppy stability that has characterized it
since the end of World War II. Such dependence itself is more and more threatening the
stability of capitalism as a system, as it also
intensifies questioning of a system which must
be enamored of death in order to live.

Inequality and Freedom

The concentration upon the purely political
carries over to the very formal nature of the
idea of equality in bourgeois freedom. Here
the equality was a matter of law only; it did
not extend fully even into the political realm
insofar as those without sufficient property were
debarred from participating in the selection of
state officers or from holding office. In addition,
in bourgeois theory, the existence of inequality
in matters of material possession was held to be
a proof of the existence of a free government.
I do not mean to say that it was held that
the existence of rich and poor was itself proof
of the absence of tyranny; of course, this was
not the classical view, and of course it was
well known that rich and poor had existed
with political tyranny.

But it was held in classical bourgeois political theory that a free government would be
one in which ability and lack of it would have
free reign; it was also held that the presence
or absence of wealth was the basic determinant
of the existence or absence of ability. Hence,
it followed that where one had a free govern-

ment, and a natural economic order, *i.e.*, capitalism, one would have, without any inhibition, the fullest play of abilities; therefore, a free government would be one in which inequality in economic terms would be present. Economic inequality, then, was a hallmark of the existence of political freedom, which is to say freedom, for freedom was only political.

Basic, then, to the bourgeois concept of freedom were: (1) capitalism as a natural system of political economy; (2) the absence of governmental restraint; (3) the presence of restraint upon government; (4) power as essentially evil and requiring control if freedom is to exist; (5) freedom has relevance only to the political, not to the economic; (6) the existence of economic inequality as a hallmark of and a necessary consequence of freedom.

There are three more important components of the bourgeois concept of freedom that require development. These are, to state them summarily, first the idea of spontaneity as being an essential element of freedom; second, the concentration upon individualism as vital to freedom; and, third, the strain of elitism that runs through this presentation of freedom. Let us consider each of these.

Spontaneity

Spontaneity is viewed as important to freedom in the sense that when action is fortuitous it is devoid of compulsion, restraint and regulation. We speak of being as "free as the wind"; of being "free and easy." This stems from the rebellion against the regulatory character of feudalism, and from the idea of capitalism as being a natural system, functioning automatically, properly and reasonably, if only left alone. From this it is but a step to insist that spontaneity itself is of the essence of freedom. This is particularly true where, as in bourgeois theory, power itself is viewed with extreme hostility; hence, the planned or organized exercise of control or direction, the opposite of spontaneity, must be the foe of freedom.

There is, also, in the concentration upon spontaneity, a reflection of philosophical idealism with its denial of materially based and structurally induced causes as being fundamental sources accounting for economic, social, and political phenomena. This also follows quite logically from the view of capitalism as being a natural order; it has the added virtue of making absurd or irrelevant proposals for social change of a radical nature.

Individualism

The emphasis upon individualism also follows very logically from all the postulates of the bourgeois theory of freedom. If capitalism is a natural order, *laissez-faire* is proper; if *laissez-faire* is proper then it is "every man for himself," in a system that is self-adjusting and runs itself, like any other natural thing, and one must expect to "sink or swim." You must "stand on your own feet"; no one "owes you a living"; you have to "make your own pile." You may even have to be ruthless; certainly you will have to be and want to be "rugged."

Everything, then, is individually centered; the widest possible extension meriting approval is responsibility for one's family. It is not a far step from this to the glorification of one's "pleasures," and to the pursuit of such personalized pleasures as being the purpose and the end of life. Religion offers some muting of this; but even there, salvation is an individual matter.

This, too, is related to the early concept of political office as being a source of self-enrichment, something institutionalized, for instance, in 17th and 18th-century England, in the American "spoils system," and in the American meaning of the word, "politician." There is, in fact, a stark ambiguity in the whole idea of public servant in a society geared to self-enrichment as being of the essence of the organism. Related to this is the idea that failures move into areas of such service—incompetents, as teachers, for if you know you do, and if you do not know then you teach; or ministers, who are out of this world and rather effeminate anyway; and those on the public payroll, who are ne'er-do-wells and hangers-on and errand boys for the inevitable "big shots."

A rigorous presentation of this outlook was made in the work entitled *What Social Classes Owe to Each Other*, written by the eminent American sociologist, William Graham Sumner, in the late 1880's. Mr. Sumner, for many years a professor at Yale University, and perhaps best known for his book, *Folkways*, produced in the first-mentioned work (which sold very well in its day, by the way) a full-scale defense of complete individualism.

The content of Sumner's book is indicated in the reply its author made to the question posed in his title; asking what social classes owed to each other, Sumner replied: "Nothing." Back some 70 years ago, sociologists had not yet developed the sophisticated approach of denying the existence of classes, so Sumner accepted this as universally understood. But he was troubled by the wave of radicalism, liberalism and "do-goodism" that appeared here, especially after the "Long Depression" of 1873-79. And he undertook to show that given the natural and inevitable quality of capitalism, any tampering with the way in which wealth was distributed, or any infringement upon the absolute inviolability of property rights was utterly wrong-headed and could lead only to disaster. The poor were poor because they were inefficient, or stupid, or otherwise defective; and the rich were rich because they were the opposite of the poor. Any attempt to undo the working of nature in the economic and social spheres would result in increased suffering, would be unjust, and could only be highly transitory because no matter what was done artificially, ability and quality would tell and fairly soon the rich would be rich again and the poor would be poor again.

It is this kind of thinking which made the misapplication of Darwinism to society so attractive to adherents of capitalism and produced a Social-Darwinism whose history has been ably chronicled by James Bert Loewenberg and others. Relevant, also, is the considerable vogue of Ayn Rand's novels and tracts, and the appearance of something approaching a "movement" for the philosophy of supreme and dedicated selfishness.

At the other end of the bourgeois range in politics from Ayn Rand—that is, at the liberal, rather than the conservative end—the individualism and the riches assumed as necessary for "freedom" were enunciated in this paragraph from Jacques Barzun, Provost of Columbia University:

"The liberal outlook is no hidden secret; it is the outlook of the man who is free, because he does not toil for his living, because his responsibilities are of his own choice, and because he can waste time in the pursuit of objects that only he values and understands. Few institutions have come near this kind of freedom."*

Elitism

A logical extension of all this is a firm commitment to elitism. Elitism is basic to dominant thinking wherever class-stratification exists. In capitalism it is especially strong, because there nature allegedly has triumphed and so those who are on top must be on top not because of caste or inheritance or other artificial contrivances, but because of superior ability. Hence has been achieved the true aristocracy and the natural elite; all are supposed to be "self-made" and really the victors in a "fair contest." The elitism, so marked a feature of capitalism, is

*Quoted from *The University in America,* Occasional Paper, Center for the Study of Democratic Institutions, Santa Barbara, 1967, p. 27.

further intensified by the racism that has been associated with the development and growth of capitalism, and especially with present-day capitalism or imperialism.

Capitalism in fact has been characterized by this dual elitism. There is, first, the internal, where those who possess the means of production and who effectively dominate the society are held to be superior to the rest of the population, making up the vast majority. There is, second, the external, composed of the darker peoples of the earth (in particular instances, as in our own country, this can simultaneously be internal, too) who are referred to as the "backward" peoples.

The darker ones are to produce raw materials for sale at prices others administer and shipped in conveyances others own and marketed at prices others set; and they are not to produce finished products of their own, but rather are to purchase these from advanced areas, again under terms set by those advanced areas. These peoples, being over-exploited, are the underdeveloped; but the underdevelopment is to be charged not to the exploitation, but to themselves, and is to be a proof of their inferiority. That is, the very feature that accounts for the exploitative relationship is fastened upon as the source not of the exploitation, but of the backwardness.

With this external elitism, and its especially marked exploitation, some of the intensity of the conflicts threatening the home order may be diluted. That is, on the basis of the super-exploitation of the darker, colonial peoples, relatively higher standards may be permitted for our "own" inferior ones. And these relatively higher standards will apply not only to standards of living, but also to political practices. Pertinent is the remark made by Marx in a letter to Engels, written May 23, 1856, soon after the writer had returned from a tour of Ireland: "One can already notice here that the so-called liberty of English citizens is based on the oppression of the colonies."

It is not coincidental that the development of bourgeois democracy in the direction of enfranchisement of the non-propertied occurs with the development of imperialism. The possibility of dropping some economic benefits to selected layers of the "inferior" classes at home, makes possible also the enhancement of their political rights, especially as the former process tends to develop opportunism and class collaborationism at home. Actually, the process is a highly complex one, and the basic source of both economic and political advance for working people in the home areas of imperialism lies in their own struggles, organizations, and strength. Nevertheless, the possibility of yielding and the policy of concession, and the development of a kind of "unity" of classes, are also closely tied in with the benefits of imperialism, so far as the elite is concerned.

By the same token, the breakup of imperialism is enhanced by the simultaneous cracking of both layers of elitist domination. That is, the revolt of the darker peoples complements the internal conflicts; their intensification in turn inspires a swifter pace in the external.

The essential point, for present purposes, is the fact that "freedom" in bourgeois theory and practice has been basically elitist and racist. It always has carried with it something of the wolf's "freedom" to eat the sheep; the freedom of the former is the death of the latter. In this fundamental manner, the freedom-concept in bourgeois theory and practice always has had about it a certain anti-humanistic essence, understandable, of course, in a theory expressive of the limitations of a social order still confined to the pre-human epoch of history.

4. The Marxist Concept of Freedom

In contrast to the bourgeois theory of freedom, the Marxist does not view it negatively, but, rather, positively. That is, while the bourgeois theory of freedom focuses upon the absence of restraint upon the individual, and the presence of restraint upon the government, in terms of what it may *not* do, the focus of the Marxist theory is opposite. It tends to view freedom not so much in terms of what may not be done, but rather in terms of what can be and should be done.

The negative quality of the bourgeois theory springs from its view of capitalism as a natural and altogether salutary system—as, indeed, that ordering of society in which reason has triumphed and therefore one in which the laws of nature are in operation. Under such circumstances, the less done the better; in this case, prohibitions against the state are of the essence of assuring freedom. This, it is of the utmost importance to remember, assumed the private ownership of the means of production, and the safeguarding of that relationship as the essential function of the state and as the hallmark of a civilized society.

The State and Power

In this sense, the state, so far as the propertied classes are concerned, is an evil; it is necessary, however, in terms of restraining the non-propertied, those outside the ken of politics, and in terms of international intercourse.

The Marxist view is altogether different. It sees capitalism not as natural and beneficent, but as artificial and parasitic. It sees capitalism as a progressive *force*, relative to the feudalism it displaces, but not as a progressive *system*, because of its class nature and its exploitative essence. The Marxist view holds that the private ownership of the means of production, to be carefully distinguished from other forms of property, far from being a hallmark of civilization, is the fundamental constituent of pre-human history; and that, especially with the intensified socializing of the productive process, the retention of the individualized mode of appropriation becomes more and more stultifying, not only economically, but also socially, ethically, and psychologically.

Hence, the Marxist view of the state is class-oriented. The Marxist agrees with the classical bourgeois approach which sees the protection of private property ownership as basic to the function of the state; but evaluating such ownership in terms exactly the opposite of those of the bourgeoisie, the Marxist sees this commitment on the part of the state as the root of its evil quality. The Marxist, seeking the transformation of that property relationship, simultaneously seeks the transformation of the nature of the state from an organ for its preservation into an organ for its elimination. In the former case, given the idea of the naturalness of the economic foundation, the whole point of freedom will be the absence of restraint; in the latter case, given the idea of the exploitative nature of the economic foundation, the whole point in the effort to achieve freedom will be the active searching for the means of altering that foundation.

The bourgeoisie, having rebelled against feudalism and autocracy and having achieved, in its own mind, the final Elysium of a reasonable social order, in conformity with natural laws and rewarding merit and penalizing its absence, will be exceedingly suspicious of power *per se;* it will view political power as a possible threat to its own order.* The Marxist views power also in class terms and sees it as being used to maintain capitalism, the system giving power its

*On the other hand there is a dialectics at work here, too; thus, where the bourgeoisie feels itself incapable of ruling in the old way it may turn to fascism—i.e., the unbridled use of state power to prevent its demise. In doing this, however, the bourgeoisie explicitly renounces freedom, democracy, equality and rationalism—i.e., the slogans and attributes of its birth and youth.

particular content But the Marxist does not take a hostile or necessarily suspicious view of power *per se;* it depends upon what kind of power, with what source, and used for what ends.

Freedom—Political and Economic

The bourgeoisie views freedom as a concept having only political content; it considers economic matters as irrelevant to problems of freedom. This is because for the bourgeoisie, as we have emphasized, capitalism is not really an economic system but is rather a natural order. Capitalism *is,* for the bourgeoisie, economic freedom; its retention requires only non-interference with its natural functioning. There have been all sorts of compromises of this pure view, of course, in the recent past; but these compromises reflect the fact that capitalism, being in general crisis, is therefore doctoring its ideology and its practice. The compromises do not negate the reality of the basic assumption of bourgeois theory relative to the non-economic nature of freedom concepts.

The Marxist insists upon the artificial, manmade, and historically-derived character of capitalism; he, therefore, insists that coercion, not freedom, characterizes the economics of capitalism. Furthermore, the Marxist views the economic substratum of a social order as ultimately decisive for its nature; he, therefore, holds that the existence of class divisions, the organization of society on the basis of those who own and those who do not own the means of production, assures the domination of society by the owners, and the subordination in society of the ownerless.

Hence, while in bourgeois theory, freedom has only a political meaning and no relevance to economic matters, in Marxist theory the economic relations fundamentally determine societal characteristics and content and therefore these relations have the closest connection with the question of freedom. The problem of freedom to the Marxist is human and therefore societal; it is not simply political. The Marxist view being dialectical is never compartmentalized; therefore, in freedom, as in everything else, it sees the question as a unity and as a whole, not as an abstraction and as a part.

On Equality

Bourgeois theory sees economic inequality as an attribute of a free society. While, at its finest, this theory insists that "all men are created equal," this insistence is political, legal, formal. It is an insistence that in matters of the polity, and in matters of the law, no man, because of wealth, descent, or for any other reason, was to have an advantage (politically, legally) over another man. It is to be noted, in the first place, that even within formal, political, and legal limits, this idea, when first enunciated in 1776, ruled out women, and meant only white men, and in the latter instance meant free white men, not those held in indenture. And even with free white men, it admitted political inequality in the existence of discriminatory legislation from an economic and religious point of view. But leaving aside these exceptions, important as they are, and accepting in full the phrase as written, bourgeois equality, like bourgeois freedom, has application only to the political.

But, political equality deriving out of the naturalness of the economy, assured the coming into being of economic inequality. This inequality, the result of differing abilities, was, then, a hall-mark of a free society. Even among the most enlightened and most revolutionary of the bourgeois democrats, like Jefferson, who tended to fear the appearance of too sharp economic inequalities as threatening the stability of society, what they desired was not the elimination of such inequality but its muting and, at most, its limitation.

In Marxist theory, economic inequality is viewed as an attribute of an unfree society. The emphasis upon the economic as at the root of societal reality and as at the heart of actual power, naturally would lead to the condemnation of economic inequality as being violative of freedom. While, then, Marxism is not equalitarian in the sense of anarchism—where there is no allowance for the development of such technical and economic proficiency as to allow abundance, nor for incentive prior to the achievement of the possibility of such abundance and during the transition from capitalism to communism—still Marxism is basically equalitarian. It does view significant divergence in income with suspicion, and it does see this as fundamentally reflective of the still limited techniques and ethics of socialism; and it sees its elimination as one of the distinguishing features of communism as contrasted with socialism.

Individualism

The individualism so heavily emphasized by bourgeois theory is suspect in Marxist theory. The suspicion has two roots: (1) that the individualism is fundamentally a luxury of those who own the means of production and has in it more irresponsibility and hedonism than any real effort to develop the potential or the creativity of the individual human being; (2) that the individualism partakes of the cannibalistic and is in conflict with the highly socialized nature of modern life. From these considerations flow the attributes that C. Wright Mills described: "the U.S.A. [is] an overdeveloped society full of ugly waste and the deadening of human sensibility, honoring ignorance and the cheerful robot, pronouncing the barren doctrine and submitting gladly, even with eagerness, to the uneasy fun of a leisureless and emptying existence." Mills does not differentiate enough in his description of our society, especially in class terms, but I think no perceptive person will deny the large element of truth in his analysis.

Furthermore, the individualism conflicts with the collective needs of society; more and more, therefore, practice departs from principle. This, in turn, arouses fierce feelings of guilt and of ennui or cynicism, which help induce anti-social patterns of behavior and multiplying cases of breakdown.

The Marxist view of human beings generally

is an optimistic one; the dominant bourgeois outlook is rather gloomy. It is true that the bourgeoisie in its revolutionary youth, when it sought to remake the world, tended to take a very positive approach to people, expressed most beautifully and exuberantly by Shakespeare who, it will be remembered, compared man to a veritable god. But the bourgeoisie, when it saw man as noble, meant men of property, men of propriety, men who mattered. And the strain that sees man as damned and as a worm, which runs through the entire record of class-divided history, is never wholly absent from the bourgeois literature. It becomes increasingly important, as do so many other attributes of medievalism, with capitalism's decline.

Marxism insists upon the corrupting quality of class society, not the corrupt quality of human beings. Moreover, while bourgeois theory assumes the enervating effect of impoverishment and oppression, Marxism insists upon the corroding influence of class domination and the ennobling influence of common struggle. The bourgeoisie tends to see the debilitating effect of victimization; Marxism sees the victim, but does not see him as passive, and sees his struggle as continual and creative.

To the bourgeoisie, to have had ancestors who were slaves is shameful; to have had ancestors who were slaveowners is a mark of distinction, and the more numerous their slaves, the greater the distinction. The Marxist's evaluations are opposite.

Marxism and Elitism

All class-divided societies, and notably capitalism, have taken a basically elitist view of civilization. All of them, reflecting the domination of the majority by a minority, have developed theories justifying such an arrangement. These theories, whether of a religious or a secular guise, in fact have held that the rule by the few was necessary and proper because the many were the inferior (or the more sinful) of the few. In capitalism it is insisted that the minority who possess the means of production obtain and retain that possession as a result of superior ability and that therefore the elitism is really a natural expression of capacity.

This may be justified ideologically by the insistence that the few are the Elect, religiously speaking, or that the few are the more intelligent, psychologically and "scientifically" speaking. For the latter purpose, developed in our more secular age, so-called intelligence tests are concocted, and corrupted, misapplied and misinterpreted to demonstrate—to no one's surprise and to the elite's comfort—that the well-to-do are the bright ones and the poor are the stupid ones.

Inferentially, the results on the tests explain the positions in society, while, in fact, the tests are based upon the stratifications in society, and the whole method of testing and grading and interpreting reflects the same stratification. And so each explains the other, and all is right in the best of all possible worlds. Then the educational system is geared in accordance with the findings; thus again assuring that similar findings will recur, and also assuring, it is hoped, the continuance of the status quo that produced the original findings in the first place.

These are some of the main ideological trappings for the internal elitism of capitalism, which, in essentials, go back more or less unchanged to the beginnings of recorded history. The venerable nature of the theory, by the way, gives it additional authority.

With capitalism's expansion come the colonialism of the 17th and 18th centuries and the imperialism of the 19th and 20th centuries. Both widen and deepen capitalism's exploitation, and both bring the rulers of capitalism into collision with differing societies and peoples. These societies are to be undone and their peoples exploited; both distasteful undertakings beg for rationalization, especially in view of their apparent contradiction with religious and political ideas developed for home use in the course of anti-feudal efforts. The elitism organic to ruling-class thought is brought into play to justify this rapine and oppression; happily, the victims this time are not only of different religion and speech and custom, but also are of a different color. Hence develops the particular elitism known as racism; the internal and external elitism of the bourgeois epoch feed each other and together help mightily in sustaining the whole exploitative structure.

In fact—and to a degree, in articulated theory —the external elitism is an important source of what political freedom does develop in the homes of western capitalism. Just as John C. Calhoun insisted that only with the enslavement of the black was the freedom of the white possible, so imperialism has insisted that only with the super-exploitation and gross deprivation of the darker peoples of the world could there be any economic concessions or political reforms at home.

Marxism rejects elitism and racism root and branch. It points to their existence as vitiating bourgeois-democratic theory and practice, and it insists that the substance of the elitist theory is false. The superior capacity of the rulers in class-stratified societies in the past has been basically in the areas of domination, guile, and deception; and the superior position has reflected domination of the means of production and hence of the means of communication. The vast majority of human beings, deprived of the ownership of the means of production, have been the doers and the creators in all history. It is they who have produced; they have sustained the few, not the few the many.*

The superior capacity of the rich has been the capacity to rule; its possession of power has been based upon its possession of the means of production. With this domination has gone a system of elitism that has deprived and still deprives the majority of mankind of the cul-

---

*Mark Twain's *Connecticut Yankee* is expressing this morality when he says of the productive workers that, "they were the nation, the actual Nation; they were about all of it that was useful or worth saving or really respectworthy, and to subtract them would have been to subtract the Nation and leave behind some dregs, some refuse, in the shape of a king, nobility and gentry, idle, unproductive, acquainted mainly with the arts of wasting and destroying and of no sort of use or value in any rationally constructed world."

tural, educational, political and material treasures of the world. This has meant the denial of freedom to the vast majority of humanity; on the basis of that denial, others have had varying portions and forms of freedom.

Marxism holds that these treasures, produced by the labor of the deprived majority, belong really to them, and that they are fully capable, given the opportunity, of enjoying them. Marxism holds that the vast majority, coming into effective possession of the means of production, will be able to overcome—have already in fact overcome, in the lands of Socialism in varying degrees—what Marx called "the realm of necessity." On this basis, having provided a sufficiency of the needs of mankind, is it then possible to create, in Marx' words, "a real realm of freedom." Then will be forged a communist society in which the fullest freedom of self-expression in all spheres of human activity, and none colliding with the others' self-expression, will exist.

Then will appear, for the first time, a society on earth in which the vast majority are literate, cultured, secure, healthy and fraternal; this will make possible such a renaissance of culture and such a growth of human capacity as has never yet even been dreamed.

On Spontaneity and Planning

As we have noted, one of the components of freedom in the bourgeois view is spontaneity. Somehow, only the unforetold can be free. Marxism's view is quite otherwise.

In terms of spontaneity, what is more spontaneous than a boat in a tossing sea, with one untrained man aboard? But suppose one adds training to the man, and he employs that training. Is there not then a loss of spontaneity? But is there a loss of freedom? Is there rather not a gain in the freedom of the man, insofar as he is now more the master of his own fate than he was before? And if one gives this man, oars and sails so that he may employ his training more effectively; and adds a compass, and a map, and a motor, and a crew of well-trained men with whom he may work and who may share in the various tasks? Does not each one of these additions lessen the spontaneity and enhance the freedom?

Planning seems an intrusion where it is held that the prevailing order is self-regulating, and that nothing harms its functioning so much as interference with that self-regulation. This helps develop in capitalist society an insistence that that which is planned, having lost spontaneity, has lost freedom. But all this is based, usually without articulation, on the assumption that capitalism is a natural order and does function naturally. For in other matters no one acts in this planless and spontaneous manner. No one, for instance, would think of erecting a building without a plan; and no one would think of drawing up a plan for a building without some knowledge of the nature of materials, the laws of physics, the rules of design, etc. Such knowledge and such planning are prerequisites for the building; without them, and other things, one is not able to, or in other words, is not free to, erect the building.

Conclusion

If one structures his view of all life and society in terms of the dialectical-materialist outlook, then that which is obvious in the building of a house is equally obvious in life and society as a whole. It is infinitely more complex and difficult in the latter than in the former, but the principle is the same. This is the meaning of Engels' famous phrase that "freedom is the appreciation of necessity." "Freedom," Engels continued in his *Anti-Dühring*, "does not consist in the dream of independence of natural laws, but in the knowledge of these laws, and in the possibility this gives of systematically making them work toward definite ends." Hence, "freedom of the will means nothing but the capacity to make decisions with real knowledge of the subject."*

*(Frederick Engels *Anti-Dühring*, N. Y. 1939). Note the same idea in the writing of the great "heretic"and martyr, Giordano Bruno, who in the 16th century, held that, "Necessity and liberty are one; hence what acts by the necessity of nature acts freely." Prof. Svetozar Stojanovic, of the University of Belgrade, argues that this formulation by Engels reflects "extreme determinism," and that "real freedom is possible only within Marx's moderate determinism." I do not myself see such a distinction between Engels and Marx and find nothing "extreme" in the formulation from Engels quoted above; but I did want to call attention to Prof. Stojanovic's view. See his essay, "Marx's Theory of Ethics," in N. Lobkowicz, ed., *Marx and the Western World*, (Univ. of Notre Dame Press, 1967), pp. 161-71; quoted material from p. 169.

Hence, too, as Engels pointed out, freedom "is necessarily a product of historical development." It grows as knowledge grows. The growth of knowledge leads ever nearer to the achievement of truth; the latter objectively exists; the former is the way to it. And, in the Biblical phrase, "Know ye the truth, and the truth shall make ye free." Stripping the word truth of its religious quality, of its dependence upon faith; secularizing it, and making it depend upon science, one has the path toward the achievement of freedom, in the Marxist view.

5. On The Nature of Revolution

We may begin our examination of the nature of revolution with the question of whether or not such an inquiry is relevant to our era. We say this for some have insisted that revolution is outmoded in the present epoch. Professor Arthur M. Schlesinger, Jr., for example, in his book, *The Vital Center,* published in 1949, expressed the opinion that "modern science has given the ruling class power which renders mass revolutions obsolete."* That Mr. Schlesinger

---

*At times this thought is amended to read that such revolutions have become 'obsolete" in the West. Thus, George Lichtheim: "while the bourgeois revolution is over in the West, the proletarian revolution has turned out to be an impossibility. . . ." Since recent political considerations have dictated that Greece and Turkey

chose to write this at the very moment when the revolution of the Chinese people had achieved success reflects more than bad timing; it indicates a fundamental misjudgment of the nature of our time and the nature of social revolution.

Surely, the years since 1949—one need only think of the revolutions in Egypt, Viet Nam, Iraq, and Cuba—have demonstrated the absurdity of the idea that because of the developments of technique, or for any other reason, mass revolutions have been rendered obsolete. On the contrary, we are living in an era when the obsolescence of a social order, capitalism, in its imperialist stage, has put revolution on the agenda. We are living, in fact, in the century that is characterized by the transformation of the world from an imperialist-dominated one to a socialist one; this is just as certain as it is certain that, some five hundred years ago, the peoples of Western civilization were living in a time characterized by the transition from feudalism to capitalism.

The developments of improved techniques of destruction and propaganda in the hands of the ruling classes have made necessary some alterations in the tactics of revolution; but, as the events of every passing day confirm, they have not eliminated the process of revolution.

---

are North Atlantic powers, perhaps similar considerations require some scholars to place Cuba in the "East"! The Lichtheim quotation is from his essay, "On the Interpretation of Marx's Thought," in N. Lobkowicz, ed., *Marx and the Western World*, p. 4.

Indeed, our era is the era of revolution par excellence, without precedent in history for the substantive nature of its transforming force, for the quantitative sweep which encompasses whole continents rather than single nations, and for the speed with which it unfolds.

Definitions of "Revolution"

How shall we define this term, "revolution"? The dictionary offers this: "A sudden and violent change in government or in the political constitution of a country, mainly brought about by internal causes." In this definition I find very little with which to agree, though the emphasis upon internal causes as being of prime consequence is valid, I believe. I would rather define revolution as an historical process leading to and culminating in social transformation, wherein one ruling class is displaced by another, with the new class representing, as compared to the old, enhanced productive capacities and socially progressive potentialities. This definition is to be preferred to the other, it seems to me, on many grounds; one is that with the dictionary definition there is no distinction between revolution and counter-revolution. But in my view these are two quite distinct, indeed, opposite phenomena, and any definition that would call both the victory of George Washington and the victory of Francisco Franco by the same name is bound to confuse more than define.

The history of mankind is a remarkably dynamic one; change is one of its few constants, including the recurring appearance of changes of such consequence and of such a nature that only the term "revolution," as I have defined it, correctly characterizes them.

When one stops to think about this, it is very nearly miraculous. For consider: Every exploitative ruling class, in the past, everywhere in the world, throughout the thousands of years of recorded history, has held in its hands, since it was the ruling class, effective domination of the society. It has, to begin with, owned the means of production; it has dominated the state apparatus; and it has dominated, also, the ideology and the culture of the society. In certain cases, as, for example, in systems of chattel slavery, ruling classes actually have possessed physically not only the natural and man-made means of production, but also the human producers themselves.

Class Rule Versus Change

At first glance, surely one would think that such arrangements would defy basic alteration. Where classes control production, communication, education, law, and ideology in general, and the whole state apparatus with its facilities for persuasion and repression, does it not appear that the easiest thing to do would be to maintain such a system? It is no wonder, then, that every exploitative ruling class in the past has insisted that its system, or "way of life," was splendid and manifestly destined to last forever. But it *is* a wonder that though every ruling class, in every epoch, everywhere in the world, has insisted upon this "common-sense" view, they have all, everywhere, in time, been proven wrong.

If revolution were to occur once or twice in human history, it might be explained in terms of "accident," or some notably irresponsible or inefficient conduct on the part of the particular rulers thus overthrown. But where revolution is the rule, historically speaking, despite all the manifest and not so manifest odds against its attempt, not to speak of its success, would it not appear that there must be some central explanation for this? Would it not appear that there must be some irresistible force, working within all hitherto existing social systems which, despite the apparent omnipotence of the rulers, succeeds in terminating their rule and basically altering those systems?

The Roots of Revolution

What, then, shall we say as to the source of this repeated process of revolution? It is due, I think, in the first place, to fundamental and immutable contradictions, or antagonisms, which hitherto have characterized all exploitative social systems. These manifest themselves in the fact that class conflict or class struggle makes up the fundamental dynamic of recorded history, and in that sense represents, as Marx and Engels stated, in *The Communist Manifesto*, "the history of all hitherto existing society."

Central is held to be the contradiction between the means of production and the relations of production. The former—given private ownership—is antagonistic to the latter which must be social; and as the latter develop, their social essence also develops thus bringing to a more and more critical stage the organic contradiction. The private motivation and the public function in capitalist production intensify as the latter grows, becomes more centralized and monopolized; finally the inhibiting, anti-human and parasitic qualities compel transformation of the relationship to accord with the means.

A basic theme in Marx is this inextricable contradiction between means of production and relations of production; he emphasized also that capitalism, hastening the improvement in the means, thereby tended to accentuate the process of revolution.

In the *Communist Manifesto*, Marx and Engels noted that, "The bourgeoisie cannot exist without continually revolutionizing the instruments of production, and thereby the relations of production and all the social relations."

In the first volume of *Capital* (cited edition, p. 487), Marx referred to "this absolute contradiction between the technical necessities of Modern Industry, and the social character inherent in its capitalistic form." And again (p. 488), "the historical development of the antagonisms, immanent in a given form of production, is the only way in which that form of production can be dissolved and a new form established."

Here are three more examples of this basic concept in Marxism, all again from the masterwork, *Capital*:

"By maturing the material conditions, and

the combination on a social scale of the processes of production, it matures the contradictions and antagonisms of the capitalist form of production, and thereby provides, along with the elements for the formation of a new society, the forces for exploding the old one" (p. 503).

". . . Within the capitalist system . . . all means for the development of production transform themselves into means of domination over, and exploitation of, the producers; they mutilate the laborer into a fragment of a man, degrade him to the level of an appendage of a machine, destroy every remnant of charm in his work and turn it into a hated toil; they estrange from him the intellectual potentialities of the labor-process in the same proportion as science is incorporated in it as an independent power . . . It follows, therefore, that in proportion as capital accumulates, the lot of the laborer, *be his payment high or low*, must grow worse" (p. 645, italics added).

Finally, and directly: "Centralization of the means of production and socialization of labor at last reach a point where they become incompatible with their capitalist integument. This integument is burst asunder. The knell of private property sounds. The expropriators are expropriated" (p. 763).

This contradiction is organic to the society's nature; hence, the process of revolution is part of the process of the very life and development of the society itself. Hence, too, ruling classes, be they as apparently all-powerful as they please, never have been able in the past to prevent their own demise.

At the same time, the contradiction does not manifest itself simply in the decay of the efficacy of the ruling class; it manifests itself, also, in the rising strength, consciousness, and organization of those being ruled. This two-sided feature of the contradiction is reinforcing; it is interpenetrating, each serving simultaneously as cause and effect, as stimulant and result. That is, the relationship between the two elements of the contradiction is dialectical.

This internal contradiction is of basic consequence in explaining the process of revolution. In addition, there is an external contradiction, as it were, which exists in the fact of the uneven development of all hitherto existing social systems. It is a fact that no one system, at an identical stage of development, has ever dominated the globe, nor even such substantial sections of the globe that it has not been in proximity to other social systems, or essentially similar social systems but at different levels of development. This condition produces conflict and antagonism, also, particularly since each of the differing systems or levels is itself parasitic and exploitative. Such external conflict tends to bring pressures to bear upon existing social orders already beset with internal struggles. Again, here, each tends to stimulate the other; that is, the external conflict may exacerbate the internal, or the internal may precipitate the external. The relationship here, as elsewhere, is not simple and need not be direct, and ruling classes are not devoid of capabilities, including the capacity to use external challenges as lightning rods for internal difficulties. But, on the whole, uneven development with resultant conflict tends to intensify the internal contradictions besetting and finally undoing exploitative ruling classes.

With most of the human race still impoverished and illiterate, Marxism sees the overcoming of hunger and illiteracy as fundamental aspects of the problem of achieving freedom. A quite remarkable letter from a Roman Catholic priest in the lay Catholic weekly, *Commonweal* (June 30, 1967), makes this point as vigorously as any Communist has ever done. Reverend Thomas R. Melville writes from Guatemala: "Hatred or fear of Communism is not a very prevalent feeling where hunger and misery exist, certainly not as prevalent as hatred and fear of hunger and misery themselves can be."

And directly to the question of freedom, this priest writes—and lengthy quotation is merited: "The U.S. proclaims itself the defender of freedom. Freedom from what, or for what? It talks about the free peoples of the world. In what sense are they free? Free to work where they want? No, because there are no jobs. Free to live where they want? No, because they haven't even the food for life itself. Free to say what they want? No, because they can't raise their voices in protest against their exploiters without being jailed for Communism. Free to think what they want? No, because they've never even had the opportunity of schooling. Freedom for what? God knows."

An Illustration From American History

In an effort to illuminate the sources of the revolutionary process, let us turn to the history of our own country and, particularly, to the Second American Revolution—the Civil War, which completed some of the tasks of our First Revolution.

To comprehend the sources of that war, which culminated as revolution, it is necessary to understand what forces drove the dominant elements in the slaveholding class to choose the path of an attempted counter-revolutionary *coup;* for the Civil War, *in origin,* was an attempted counter-revolution. There is a considerable literature that seeks to make the villain of the piece in this instance Abraham Lincoln, and to insist that he inveigled the rulers of the South into resorting to force—just as, by the way, there is a body of literature that insists Franklin Delano Roosevelt goaded the Imperial Japanese government into bombing Pearl Harbor and, therefore, was the real precipitator of World War II, so far as U.S. involvement is concerned.

Both schools of thought are in error. As for the launching of the Civil War, with which alone we shall deal here, the evidence is overwhelming that the secession movement was plotted by leaders of the slaveholding class for months—in the case of some individuals, for years—prior to the bombing of Fort Sumter. The evidence is overwhelming that these leaders carried out, illegally and against the will of the majority of white Southerners (let alone, the will of the one-third of the population of the South which was Negro), the creation of a so-called Confederate States of America, mustered an army, and ordered contingents of that army to take over arsenals, post-offices, army centers and naval bases belonging to the United States. The evidence is conclusive, also, that these same leaders caused the bombardment of one of the forts which refused to yield, and that, as a result, for several days Fort Sumter was subjected to the force and violence of the Confederate rulers.

The Slaveholders' Counter-Revolution

The first problem, then, in connection with the source of the Civil War is to understand why the effective leadership of the slaveholding class took this course. They took this path because they had become desperate; they had decided that they had everything to gain and nothing to lose by resorting to counter-revolutionary violence. In the past, when exploitative ruling classes have become convinced that they could not maintain their rule in the old way, they have resorted, when they had the power, to the path of organized violence, that is, to the path of counter-revolution.

The dominant slaveholders in the United States resorted to this in 1860 because they came to the conclusion that if they did not, they would be undone, legally and constitutionally, in the near future. Hence, they calculated, by resorting to counter-revolution, they might succeed in thwarting or significantly delaying their burial which, they were convinced, would be their fate if they abided by the results of the 1860 elections.

There were four interpenetrating forces—two essentially internal, and two essentially external—which together drove the dominant elements in the slaveholding class to the desperate expedient of war. These were, to state them summarily first, and then to return for a brief elaboration of each of them: (1) the mounting unrest of the four million Negro slaves and the rising class consciousness and discontent of the majority of non-slaveholding whites in the south; (2) the intensifying contradictions within the economic and social system of plantation slavery itself which drove it towards a voracious expansionism; in turn, this helped precipitate the fundamental questions of the future of the federal lands and the right or wrong of the institution of slavery; (3) the socio-economic transformation north of the Mason-Dixon Line which basically threatened slaveocratic domination over the federal government; and (4) the quantitative and qualitative growth of Abolitionism.

We turn to the briefest elaboration of each of these elements. The developing discontent of the slave and non-slaveholding whites in the South reached such a crescendo in the 1850's that the slaveowners actually feared, as they said, the breaking out of civil war at home before they could launch it upon Washington. Slave revolts and plots reached a high point in the decade 1850-1860; other evidences of slave unrest, such as flight, reached extraordinary levels in the same period; examples of white participation in and sympathy toward such freedom efforts on the part of the slaves became increasingly frequent in this same decade; and, on the part of the non-slaveholding whites, political and economic organization and demands counter to the interests of the planter class became characteristic of domestic southern politics in the decade prior to secession. This ferment at home was of great significance in creating a sense of desperation on the part of the slaveholding class.

Intensified contradictions within the slave system showed themselves in the rising percentage of whites who were forced out of the slaveholding class in the years just before the Civil War, and in the mounting pressure for new lands with which to increase holdings and further productivity so that the rate of profit might not fall. It also was evident in the continuing compulsion toward expansion, deriving from the necessity to keep the proportion of Negro population to white population at a manageable level. If the area of slavery were ever thoroughly confined, the slaveholders feared, with good reason, that the problem of policing the slaves would become so great as to be self-defeating.

These together constituted fundamental internal contradictory pressures that were challenging the viability of the American slave system. In addition, outside the slave area, the North and West were being transformed by the enormous increase of a free-labor agricultural population, and by the swift rise of industrial capitalism and the growing split among the mercantile bourgeoisie in the North. As to the latter, they had earlier been engaged, especially in New York City, in servicing the planters. But as industry and wheat and corn production developed in the North and gained worldwide markets, a considerable portion of the Northern merchant class switched its prime efforts to transporting and selling free-labor-produced commodities. This change was of great importance in causing a split in the Democratic Party, generally the preferred party of the slaveowners. Thus, a Northern and a Southern Democratic Party finally became crystallized and each ran a candidate in 1860, allowing Lincoln to emerge the victor though running on a relatively new ticket, and receiving a minority of the votes.

The interests of the classes evolving as a result of this transformation—farmers, workers, industrialists, certain of the merchants—were contrary to those of the slaveowners. These clashing interests manifested themselves in conflicting positions on basic questions of the time —homestead, tariff, internal improvements at federal expense, currency and credit questions, matters of foreign policy. The 1860 defeat, therefore, represented a crushing blow to the slaveocracy and precipitated its act of desperation.

Finally, in considerable part stimulated by the development already sketched, the Abolitionist Movement, a bona-fide revolutionary movement, shed its sectarianism and became a real mass movement. It became politically alert, organizationally responsible and, in much of the North, the decisive balance of power politically and a real force ideologically. This development further terrified the slaveowners and, together with everything else, led them to attempt counter-revolution; that is, to seek the destruction of the bourgeois-democratic republic and to make permanent, if not supreme, the institution of chattel slavery on the North American continent.

These internal and external forces together drove the regressive class to violence. The republic was defended, with great vacillation and hesitation, by a coalition of classes more or less hostile to the pretensions of the slaveowners and more or less devoted to the bourgeois-democratic republic. The defense, given the multi-class nature of the coalition, was based on the broadest possible demand—defend the Union, save the Republic! At first, for purposes of unity and cohesion, it was insisted that the question of slavery was irrelevant to the conflict. But, since the ownership of four million slaves was basic to the very definition of the class mounting the counter-revolution, and since it was fundamental to the power of that class, if the assault was to be turned back it was necessary to attack the institution of slavery. Hence, defending ancient liberties—the integrity of the republic, the sanctity of legal and constitutional procedures—under new conditions, that is, under conditions which saw those liberties being assaulted in an organized manner, it became necessary to forge new freedoms. Thus, to preserve the Union it was necessary to liberate the slaves; to liberate the slaves, it was necessary to preserve the Union.

With that shift in strategy, the tactical course of the struggle shifted; Negroes, straining to get into the battle were at last allowed to do so, and before Lee surrendered 250,000 Negro men had fought in Lincoln's Army and Navy and had been of decisive consequence in producing that surrender.

Here, then, in the actualities of U.S. history, was the unfolding of the revolutionary process, to be institutionalized in the 13th and 14th Amendments to the Constitution, confiscating without compensation over three billion dollars worth of private property and laying the groundwork for the continuing effort to achieve real freedom on the part of the Negro masses.*

6. Revolution, Violence and Democracy

A. Violence

Probably the single most common stereotype in connection with revolution is to equate it with violence. Examples of this abound; the reader will recall that the dictionary definition of revolution began with the words: "A sudden and violent change in government . . ." Equally common is the posing of peaceful change as contrasted with revolution; for instance, in Kenneth Neill Cameron's introduction to the *Selected Poetry and Prose of Shelley*, the editor summarizes certain of Shelley's views this way: "In

---

*For a fuller development of this analysis of the U.S. Civil War, see the present writer's *The American Civil War* (International Publishers, N. Y., 1961).

regard to the existing situation in England the thing to do is to work first for the reform of parliament, peacefully if possible, by revolution if necessary."

But the equating of violence with the nature and process of revolution is not correct. Violence may or may not appear in such a process, and its presence or absence is not a determining feature of the definition. How, then, should one view the relationship of violence to revolution?

First, there is the historical view, the view conveyed in Marx's famous observation that "force is the midwife of every old society which is pregnant with the new." This observation, however, is not advocacy; it is observation. It is taking account of the fact—certainly a fact when Marx was writing—that hitherto social changes sufficiently fundamental to be called revolutions had not occurred peacefully. It is, also, an observation which rules out the adoption of pacifism as an ideology suitable for a revolutionary, but it most certainly does not constitute the advocacy of violence by the revolutionary himself.*

---

*Not only is it true that in this passage, Marx was referring to past history and—to be exact—to the history of the bourgeoisie; in addition, Marx was using the word "force" as synonymous with state power. The passage occurs in the first volume of *Capital*, where Marx is commenting on "different factors of primitive accumulation." He continues: "These methods depend in part on brute force, e.g., the colonial system. But they all employ the power of the State, the concentrated and organized force of society, to hasten, hot-house fashion, the process of transformation of the feudal mode of production into the capitalist mode, and to shorten the transition. Force is the midwife of every old society pregnant with the new one. It is itself an economic power."

That it does not, follows from an examination of the full content of the historical observation anent the relationship between violence and revolution. That observation insists that where violence has accompanied revolutionary culmination, it has appeared because the old class, facing elimination due to social development, has chosen to postpone its internment by resorting to the violent suppression of the challenging classes and forces. The source of the violence, when it appears, is in reaction; it is in response to that challenge that resistance may be offered and if such resistance is successful then the revolutionary process may come to fruition.

Exactly this course marks the American Revolution, where the colonists pled peacefully for a redress of grievances and for the "rights of Englishmen." These demands were resisted and the rights were not granted by the Crown. As the demands persisted, and the organized strength of the movement making those demands grew, the Crown finally moved, in 1775, to the massive, forcible suppression of the entire movement. It was for this purpose that the King ordered ten thousand troops to Boston, blockaded the port, and sent detachments of those troops, bayonets fixed, to arrest the leaders of that movement. The use of force came first as an expression of policy by the Crown; the revolutionists turned to force as a last resort and as an act of resistance to the prior-offered force by reaction. The resistance finally was successful and so the revolution proceeded. Or, as in the case of modern Spain, the effort to secure in that suffering country a republic with an advanced bourgeois-democratic system was met by the organized force and violence of feudal and fascistic groups both in Spain, and in Germany and Italy. There, the movement toward significant social change was met by reactionary violence and the resistance to that violence was not successful; hence, Franco's counter-revolutionary assault succeeded, and Spain's crucifixion continues.

Where one has a complete absence of any possibility of struggle for social progress other than through violence, he has an altogether different situation. This, for example, was true in the slave south in our own country. The slaves were forbidden all rights and were, in fact, the property of the master class. They were forbidden to learn to read and write; they were forbidden to own anything or go anywhere or do anything without the express permission of the masters. In such cases, individual resistance could only show itself in flight or being "uppity," as the masters put it, or in desperate acts of violence. And in such a system, organized struggle could only take the form of strikes, sabotage, or—and this was quite common—conspiracy and insurrection. But even here, the point I am insisting upon in connection with the relationship between the revolutionary process and violence is not really refuted, for in cases such as chattel slavery, the use of violence still originates with reaction. For in slavery, one has a system that is based upon the exercise of naked violence or the clear threat of its instant use. In slavery, the slaves were forcibly held in subjection, and the system of slavery was begun by the forcible enslavement of the original victims.

The slaves in an almost literal sense were what John Brown called them, that is, "prisoners of war." Here again, then, the actual source of the violence and the persistent policy of employing violence characterize the exploitative and oppressing class, not the class seeking basic social change.

A similar situation prevails with naked colonial domination and suppression and with fascism: with, for example, the condition that existed in Hitler Germany. There monopolists ruled by making war upon their own population and by the systematic imprisonment, torture, and annihilation of hundreds of thousands of those opposing fascism. Here, too, monopoly ruled not only by constant violence within, but also by a policy of constant and violent aggression without. In such a situation, where violence appears among those seeking real change, it once again appears only in response to the systematic resort to violence by the forces of reaction.

On this question of social change and violence, and the connection between this and such systems as slavery and fascism, the Russian theologian-philosopher, Nicolas Berdyaev, offered a relevant view. In his *Slavery and Freedom* (N. Y., 1944, Part 1, Chapter 2) one may read:

"Habitual time-hardened slavery may not appear to be a form of violence, while a movement which is directed to the abolition of slavery may appear to be violence. The social reformation of society is accepted as violence by those to whom a certain habitual social order has presented itself as freedom, even though it may be terribly unjust and wrong. All reforms in the position of the working classes call forth from one side of the bourgeois classes, shouts about the violation of freedom and the use of force. Such are the paradoxes of freedom in social life."

Since the source of violence rests with reaction, whether or not it will appear depends not so much upon the will to use it but rather upon the capacity to use it. This is why, in the history of Marxism, there have been differing evaluations, at different times, as to the possibilities of the peaceful or relatively peaceful transition to socialism. In the latter part of the 19th century Marx thought this might be possible in the United States, Great Britain, and Holland, largely because of the well-developed bourgeois-democratic systems prevailing there and the relative absence, then, of highly concentrated military establishments. With significant shifts in the situation, such estimates altered, as when, during World War I, and its intense militarization, Lenin asserted that peaceful transition was impossible. But it is to be noted that this was an estimate arising out of a consideration of the strength of reaction and its readiness and capacity to use violence. When this same Lenin thought he saw, in April 1917, a profound decay in the strength of reaction in Russia, he projected the possibility then, in Russia, of the advance peacefully to socialism.

After the February bourgeois-democratic revolution, Lenin insisted that actually two centers of power—"The Dual Power," as he called it—now existed in the country: the Provisional Government and the Soviets of Workers' and Soldiers' Deputies. The latter had faith in the honesty and good intentions of the former; and in the Soviets the Bolsheviks did not yet have a majority. The Bolsheviks believed the Provisional Government, being a bourgeois one, would not and could not really bring peace, bread, and land to the peasants; that it would persist in a war policy, in subservience to the Allies, in resisting any real agrarian or social reform and in compromising with the monarchical forces. Hence, for the Bolsheviks the need was "All power to the Soviets"; the need was to move from a bourgeois-democratic to a socialist revolution and only the latter would bring peace and desperately needed structural renovation and social enlightenment.

But it is to the point to observe that with the February revolution and for several months thereafter, Lenin dropped the slogan and tactic of "transforming the imperialist war into a civil war"; in those months he called for a policy of peaceful agitation and persuasion, for a policy of persuading the majority in the Soviets that the Bolshevik analysis was correct and in this way winning the majority and moving from bourgeois-democratic to socialist revolution.

In *Pravda,* April 7, 1917 ("The Tasks of the Proletariat in the Present Revolution," known as the "April Theses") Lenin saw three basic characteristics marking the period of transition from one to the other revolution: (1) in Russia there existed "a maximum of legally recognized rights (Russia is *now* the freest of all the belligerent countries in the world)"; (2) there was an "absence of violence against the masses"; and (3) those masses still retained "unreasoning trust" in the Provisional Government.

This being the actual situation, Lenin concluded, Bolsheviks cannot call for civil war; the need now is for explanation, patient explanation: "As long as we are in the minority we carry on the work of criticizing and exposing errors and at the same time we preach the necessity of transferring the entire state power to the Soviets. . . ."

In his "The Dual Power," published two days later, he again calls for all power to the Soviets, a change to be "made possible not by adventurist acts, but by *clarifying* proletarian minds, by *emancipating* them from the influence of the bourgeoisie." It is in this essay, also, that Lenin writes: "To become a power the class-conscious workers must win the majority to their side. *As long as* no violence is used against the people there is no other road to power . . . we dare not stand for the seizure of power by a minority."

In his pamphlet, *Letters on Tactics,* also published in April 1917, Lenin denounced above all, "any *playing* at 'seizure of power' by a workers' government . . . any kind of Blanquist adventurism." In a *Pravda* article published April 12, and entitled "A Shameless Lie of the Capitalists," the "lie" Lenin has in mind is that charging the Bolsheviks with advocacy of violence; on the contrary, Lenin writes, it is the bourgeois parties with their threats of violence and their lies about its advocacy who, in fact, are stimulating and advocating it. *"Pravda* and its followers do not preach violence. On the contrary, they declare most clearly, precisely, and definitely that our main efforts should now be concentrated on *explaining* to the proletarian masses their proletarian problems as distinguished from the petty bourgeoisie which has succumbed to chauvinist intoxication."

In a "Draft Resolution on the War," written by Lenin some time between April 15 and April 22, we find this: "Our Party will preach abstention from violence as long as the Russian capitalists and their Provisional Government confine themselves to threats of violence against the people . . . as long as the capitalists have *not* started using violence against the Soviets." This Draft Resolution, by Lenin, projected the possibility of simultaneous passage of supreme power in both Germany and in Russia to Soviets of Workers and Soldiers and that should this occur the possibility of wider, perhaps world-wide transition to socialism, would appear. Thus, "if the state power in the two countries, Germany and Russia, were to pass wholly and exclusively into the hands of the Soviets of Workers' and Soldiers' Deputies, the whole of humanity would heave a sigh of relief, for then we would really be assured of a speedy termination of the war, of a really lasting, truly democratic peace among all the nations, and, at the same time, the transition of all countries to socialism."

After the Provisional Government, on April 18, announced its intention to continue Russia's participation in the imperialist war, the Resolution of the Bolshevik Central Committee, adopted April 21, 1917, stated:

"Party propagandists and speakers must refute the despicable lies of the capitalist papers and of the papers supporting the capitalists to the effect that we are holding out the threat of *civil war*. This is a despicable lie, for only at the present moment, as long as the capitalists and their government cannot and dare not use force against the masses, as long as the masses of soldiers and workers are freely expressing their will and freely electing and displacing *all* authorities—at such a moment *there must be compliance with the will of the majority of the population* and free criticism of this will by the discontented minority; should violence be resorted to, the responsibility will fall on the Provisional Government and its supporters."

On that very day, Prime Minister Lvov of the Provisional Government offered his resignation—among other reasons because, he said, his Government no longer had the confidence of the Soviets. Thereafter, especially with the July Days, when the Kerensky government violently suppressed popular demonstrations and illegalized the Bolsheviks, only then was the tactic and method advocated in the *"April Theses"*—no violence, peaceful persuasion, achievement of a majority, full rights to dissident minorities—dropped and reactionary violence was forcibly resisted with the culmination in the Great October Revolution.*

*The quotations from Lenin may be found in his *Collected Works* (Moscow, 1964), Vol. XXIV; all italics as in original. See also V. I. Lenin, *Selected Works*, 3 vols. (International Publishers, N. Y., 1967), especially Vol. 3. Note also, Lenin's "Greetings to the Hungarian Workers," May 27, 1919, where he hails the fact that Hungary's socialist revolution (at that time) "was incomparably easier and more peaceful" than Russia's. He remarks that "this last circumstance is particularly important"; that while resistance to such

It should be noted that in the post-World War II period, the Communist Parties of Spain and Portugal at times have affirmed that they saw the *possibility* of the peaceful transition to socialism —and this where fascism rules. The estimate was based on the relationship of forces in the world and in Europe; on the exceedingly precarious hold that Franco still has upon power in Spain, and the developing force of public opinion and anti-fascist organization in Portugal. Here, again, the opinion was based upon an estimate of the power of reaction to resort, effectively, to force in order to prevent its own replacement.

Related to this, is the fact that today in the United States, strikes are infrequently accompanied by violence—although it must be said that with mounting rank-and-file impatience and militancy violence offered against strikers again is becoming less rare. Yet, as a whole, strikes and picketing today are not accompanied by violence. But 30 years ago, the opposite was true; just 30 years ago, a picket line anywhere of any size and duration almost automatically meant violent assault by police or hoodlums, or others, in the employ of the bosses. The change in this matter in our time is not due to the development of tender hearts among the police or among the bosses. The change is due, basically,

---

change will be great and must be vigorously opposed, still in the period of transition from capitalism to socialism, the main thing—the "essence"—Lenin holds, "does not lie in force alone, or even mainly in force," but rather in the "organization and discipline" of the working class seeking to "remove the basis for any kind of exploitation of man by man." (V. I. Lenin, *Against Revisionism*, Moscow, 1959, pp. 499-500.)

to the alteration in the relationship of forces *vis-à-vis* organized labor and capital—it is due to the fact that 30 years ago there were perhaps six or seven million trade-unionists and today there are 17 or 18 millions. There are other reasons for this change, including the growth of class collaborationism, but this is the basic one; the bosses have the same will to smash genuine trade unionism now as they did before, but they do not have the same power or capacity—given all relationships—to do so today as they had then.

We conclude, therefore, that violence is not an organic part of the definition of the process of revolution, and that the conventional presentation which equates violence with revolution is false. And we conclude that the conventional view which places the onus for the appearance of violence in connection with basic social change upon the advocates of such change is altogether wrong; where violence does accompany revolutionary transformation, it owes its origin and takes its impulse from the forces of reaction which seek to drown the future in blood.

Most certainly, genuine revolutionists of the 20th century are not advocates of force and violence; they are advocates of fundamental social change, often faced with the organized and systematized force and violence of the supporters of outmoded and criminal social systems. A prime example of the latter are the slum-ridden, rat-infested ghettoes of "Golden America."

B. Democracy

Next to that stereotype which identifies revolution with violence, none is more widespread than that which places revolution as antithetical to democracy. One hears frequently the question of social change posed as being between two alternatives—either the democratic or the revolutionary—with the clear inference that the two are mutually exclusive. The idea of revolution as being the opposite of democracy, carries with it also the view of the revolutionary process as being fundamentally conspiratorial.

Such ideas are in line with the Hollywood version of revolution, not with the actuality. All of us have seen the "movie-spectacular," with the dastardly rebel demanding that the lovely queen yield to his awful desires, else he will permit the revolution to sweep on; if she does yield, he promises to call the whole thing off. Such films, of course, always begin with the fine-print reminder that any similarity between what the spectators are about to see and real life is purely coincidental; certainly, as a dramatization of the revolutionary process, this conventional Hollywood version has nothing to do with reality.

If the widest popular participation, at its most intense level, be basic to the meaning of democracy—and I think it is—then the whole revolutionary process and culmination, far from being contrary to democracy, represents its quintessence. And the more fundamental the nature of the revolutionary process, the more democratic it will be, the more irrelevant will be conspiracy, the more indigenous will be its roots, and the more necessary will be the deepest involvement of the vast majority of the population.

It is counter-revolution which is anti-democratic and therefore conspiratorial in character. Counter-revoltuion, hostile to the interests of the vast majority and contemptuous of the majority, elitist and exploitative, finds it necessary to operate by stealth, through deliberate deception, and with dependence upon the precipitation of violence. This is why Aaron Burr, seeking to sever the western half of the United States from the new republic and to establish his own empire, operated with but a few confederates, accumulated weapons, and based himself upon twenty pieces of silver from French and Spanish Pilates. This is why Franco, a General of the Army of the Spanish Republic, representing extremely reactionary feudalistic elements in Spain, selling out to German and Italian fascism, secretly plotted the forcible overthrow of the legally elected and popular government, and based himself upon mercenary, non-Spanish troops for the accomplishment of the purpose.

This is why the overthrow of the Mossadegh government in Iran and of the Arbenz government in Guatemala—whose programs represented popular aspirations, as their existence reflected popular support—were engineered by the Central Intelligence Agency of the United States. These are examples of truly unpopular and therefore secretive and conspiratorial, government changes (not to speak of the question of illegality and violation of sovereignty), reflecting not revolution, but counter-revolution.

The ruling-class charge of "conspiracy" hurled against revolutionary movements has the obvious inspiration of serving to condemn such movements and as a pretext for efforts to illegalize them and to persecute their advocates and adherents. The ruling-class charge of anti-democratic heard today in this country against revolutionary efforts, reflects the demagogic use of the deep democratic traditions of our land and the persistent hold these traditions have upon many millions of our compatriots.

The basic source, however, of the conventional ruling-class charge of conspiracy and sedition, usually spiced with the additional label of alien inspiration, stems from the classes' rationalization for their own domination. That is, exploitative ruling classes always insist that the orders they dominate are idyllic and that nothing but devotion and contentment characterize the people fortunate enough to live under their rule.

Hence, where significant revolutionary movements do appear, they must reflect not fundamental contradictions and antagonisms and injustices within the system, but rather the nefarious machinations of distempered individuals or of agents of a hostile foreign power. That is, the source of the unrest may be anywhere— in the blandishments of the devil, the influence of the notorious Declaration of Independence or of *The Communist Manifesto*, or the Paris Commune, or the Moscow Kremlin, or the Garrisonian sheet published in Boston, called *The Liberator*, or the anti-American schemings of Queen Victoria, or the Protocols of Zion, or the Bavarian Illuminati—but it cannot be within the social order challenged by the unrest. For, obviously, if it were there, this would question the basic conceptions of their own order so far as those dominating it are concerned, and would tend to justify the efforts at change.

This kind of thinking, furthermore, is natural for exploitative ruling classes since their inherent elitism makes them contemptuous of the masses of people. They, therefore, tend to see them as sodden robots, or unruly children, or slumbering beasts, and feel that they may be goaded into fits of temper, or duped into displays of savagery, but that no other sources for their own expressions of their own real needs and aims are possible.* In any case, with the paternalism characteristic of elitism, exploitative ruling classes tend to be certain that they know what is best for their own "people."

A stark illustration of these tendencies and attitudes, intensified by that special form of elitism known as racism, appeared in the response of American slaveowners to evidences of unrest

---

*Apt is this from *When the Wolves Howl*, the novel by Aquilino Ribeiro, contemporary Portuguese anti-fascist writer. The scene is the trial of political prisoners, and the prosecutor is speaking: "As was expected he came up with the usual reasons—that classic argument appropriate to discretionary power—namely the presumption that there was a hidden hand in any popular disturbance or, to use its legal definition, 'collective disobedience'—the hand of communist agitators. He could not admit, and refused to allow, the possibility that a revolt could begin spontaneously among the masses because they felt their interests endangered or themselves thwarted. Everything must be the work of illegal organizations, determined to disturb the happy calm of the Portuguese Eldorado of peace and plenty." (Macmillan, N. Y., 1963, p. 186.)

among the Negro slaves. Whenever such evidences appeared, the slaveowners invariably insisted that they were due to outside agitators, Northern fanatics or knaves, who had stirred up their slaves, for their own malicious or misguided reasons. The Abolitionists denied the charge and insisted that the source of the unrest of the slaves lay in slavery. They offered a dramatic proof of this idea, when they assured the slaveowners that they knew a perfect and permanent cure for slave uprisings, and one that if not adopted would simultaneously guarantee the continuance of such uprisings.

If you would eliminate slave revolts, said the Abolitionists, eliminate slavery. If the slaves are emancipated on Monday, the following Tuesday would mark the beginning of a condition which would be permanently free of slave risings; but if the slaves are not freed, then, no matter what precautions are taken uprisings would occur.

This point was hammered home, in the days of the American Revolution—which, one might think, would be lesson enough—by Benjamin Franklin in the course of a debate over taxation policy held in the Continental Congress. At this time, a delegate from Maryland remarked that he could see no reason for making any distinction among various forms of property when it came to taxing them, and that therefore he thought the principle of taxing slaves should differ in no way from the principle of taxing sheep. Franklin, getting the eye of the chairman, asked the Marylander if he would permit an interruption for the purpose of a question, which, Mr.

Franklin believed, might serve to illuminate the point being made. The Marylander granted the courtesy and Franklin propounded one of the most pregnant questions ever conceived. Noting that the Marylander could see no difference between such property as slaves and sheep, Benjamin Franklin then asked: "Can the delegate from Maryland point to a single insurrection of sheep?"

If human beings did nothing but masticate, defecate, fornicate and, when dead, dessicate, there would be, of course, no insurrection of slaves, anymore than there have been insurrections of sheep. It is, rather, the capacity to think, yearn, dream, plan, compare; to feel discontent and to project its elimination; it is the glorious insistence that life may be better than it is for ourselves and our children which is the essential content of the human in the species human being. It is this which is the overall dynamic of history, and it is the contradictions and antagonisms within hitherto existing exploitative societies that have, fundamentally, accounted for the revolutionary process which, despite everything, has existed, developed and triumphed in the past.*

The concept of democracy is born of revolution; and not least, in this connection, is our

---

*Notice that in *The Holy Family* (1845), Marx, in explaining rebellion that afflicts exploitative society, referred to "a revolt to which it is forced by the contradiction between its *humanity* and its situation, which is an open, clear and absolute negation of its humanity" (italics in original).

own American Revolution. In the 18th century the American word "Congress" reverberated through the palaces of the world with the same impact with which, in the 20th century, the Russian word "Soviet" reverberated through the mansions of the world; and the word "citizen" connoted very much the same partisanship on the side of the sovereignty of the people that the word "comrade" does today.

Today, when the fullest implementation, in every aspect, of popular sovereignty is on the historical agenda, the democratic and anti-conspiratorial character of the revolutionary process is especially clear. This is why Engels, back in March 1895, in an introduction to Marx's *The Class Struggles in France* (International Publishers, N. Y., 1964), was able to write:

"The time of surprise attacks, of revolutions carried through by small conscious minorities at the head of unconscious masses, is past. Where it is a question of a complete transformation of the social organization, the masses themselves must also be in it, must themselves already have grasped what is at stake, what they are going in for with body and soul. The history of the past fifty years has taught us that."

And, I think, the history of the years since Engels penned those words has confirmed further their truth. To conclude: the revolutionary process was the most democratic of all historical developments in the past, and in the present era, the era of the transition from capitalism to socialism, the revolutionary process remains thoroughly democratic, in inspiration, in organization, in purpose, and in mode of accomplishment.*

7. On Revolution's "High Cost"

It is widely held that while revolution may possibly bring about certain worthwhile changes, it accomplishes this at a cost in human suffering that is much too high. One hears, today, for example, statements to the effect that while revolutions in Russia and in China may have resulted in certain undeniable advances, they have come at a cost in travail that was excessive.

Concerning this, I would like to offer five points for consideration.

Estimating the Cost

First, normally those who lament the allegedly excessive cost of revolution tend to accept as valid tally-sheets of the cost, the verdicts and the reports emanating from foes of the revolution. Hence, after the generation of mis-reporting about the Russian Revolution, one found a sense of astonishment among the American people

*Note, as an example from Lenin that may be multiplied many times, this in his "Greetings to Italian, French and German Communists," written October 10, 1919: "the proletariat is perfectly well aware that for the success of its revolution, for the successful overthrow of the bourgeoisie, the sympathy of the majority of the working people (and, it follows, of the majority of the population) is *absolutely necessary*." (Lenin, *Against Revisionism*, Moscow, 1959, p. 523; Italics in original.)

when the USSR stood up against the assembled might of all Europe, led by Hitler, stopped it and, with not very much help, finally hurled it back whence it had come and beyond. Again, since 1957 and the first Sputnik, a general feeling of amazement has swept large sections of the American populace in the face of great technical achievements which manifestly reflected high levels of educational, scientific, engineering and industrial development in the Soviet Union, and which contradicted the picture they had been given of a backward, impoverished, cowed and ignorant population.

Thus, individuals like Mrs. Roosevelt and Adlai Stevenson, having returned from the USSR and being alarmed at the abysmal ignorance and misinformation concerning it that predominate in our own country, appealed for some effort at realistic reportage. At the same time he made this appeal, Mr. Stevenson hinted at something of the source of the misrepresentation when he remarked that it was difficult to tell the truth about the astonishing accomplishments in education, science, and production in the USSR without appearing to be a partisan of socialism!

When it comes to the Chinese Revolution, the U.S. Government's absurd insistence that the Chinese mainland only exists when it chooses to "recognize" it, has produced the nearly total absence of any first-hand American reportage, and to this day the *New York Times* has not even learned that the correct spelling of the capital of the Chinese People's Republic is Peking, and not Peiping!

In the face of the notoriously biased and fallacious reportage concerning revolutions, those who claim that the cost of whatever progress they may bring is too high, do depend for their estimate of that cost upon such reportage. This manifestly will not do.

The Cost of Arriving at the Status Quo

Secondly, those who lament the high cost of revolution tend, at least by implication, to assume that the cost of arriving at the status quo was low. We would urge that this needs reconsideration. There are in the world today two major kinds of revolutionary movements—often inter-related—for national liberation, and for socialism. Both are aimed at the termination of imperialism; *has the cost of producing this imperialism ever been counted up?*

Are not the African slave trade and Negro slavery associated with the beginnings and development of capitalism? Are not the genocidal policies carried out against the original inhabitants of the Americas and of Asia similarly associated? Is not the centuries' long torment of India connected with the rise of British capitalism and imperialism? Have not preparations for war and the making of war been the most lucrative businesses for capitalism for several hundreds of years? Is it not a fact that the historical developments I have just mentioned cost the lives of hundreds of millions of people through some four centuries; and might one not easily add many others, equally organic to the rise of capitalism and the truth about colonialism and imperialism, which have taken the lives

of and caused fearful suffering to additional millions upon millions of men, women, and children?

The Cost of the Status Quo

Thirdly, lamentations about the high cost of
revolution assume, do they not, that the status
quo exists at a low cost in terms of human suffering? But is this true? We have referred spe-
cifically to the Russian and Chinese revolutions,
since these are most often cited as the "horrible
examples." Very well, what of the status quo
that existed and was undone by the revolutions
there? Were not Old China and Old Russia
torn repeatedly by wars fought for sordid ends,
and taking millions of lives? Were not Old China
and Old Russia marked by mass illiteracy, by terrible epidemics, by repeated famines, by fiercely
high death rates? Were not the women in Old
China and Old Russia hardly more than slaves?
Was not the persecution of minorities on national and religious grounds institutionalized
in both? Was not prostitution rampant in those
"good old days?' Were not those countries
prime examples of terrible backwardness and impoverishment? Are these realities of the former
status quo sufficiently borne in mind by those
who "regret" the "high cost" of Revolution?*

*Relevant are these lines from the Brazilian scholar,
Helio Jaguaribe, now a professor at Stanford: "In the
Latin American countries, whatever the efforts of anti-
Communist propaganda, on the one hand, and the
awareness, on the other, of the tremendous prices to be
paid for the achievement of development by the Communist model more and more sectors of the population

Never were the advocates of the "high cost of revolution" more forthrightly rebutted than in the burning ideas Twain put into the mind of his Connecticut Yankee:

"Why, it was like reading about France and the French before the ever memorable and blessed Revolution, which swept a thousand years of such villainy away in one swift tidal wave of blood—one: a settlement of that hoary debt in the proportion of half a drop of blood for each hogshead of it that had been pressed by slow torture out of that people in the weary stretch of ten centuries of wrong and shame and misery the like of which was not to be mated but in hell. There were two 'reigns of Terror,' if we would but remember it and consider it; the one wrought murder in hot passion, the other in heartless cold blood; the one lasted mere months, the other had lasted a thousand years; the one inflicted death upon ten thousand persons, the other upon a hundred millions; but our shudders are all for the 'horrors' of the minor Terror, the momentary Terror, so to speak, whereas what is the horror of swift death by the ax compared with life-long death from hunger, cold, insult, cruelty, and heart-break? What is swift death by lightning compared with death by slow fire at the stake? A city cemetery could contain

---

are being led to conclude that this model at least affords reliable prospects of success, if and when all the other alternatives prove to be ineffective. *Furthermore they have come to understand that the highest price for development is cheaper than the price for no development at all.*" In an essay, "Marxism and Latin American Development," in N. Lobkowicz, ed., *Marx and the Western World*, p. 245, italics added.

the coffins filled by that brief Terror which we have all been so diligently taught to shiver at and mourn over, but all France could hardly contain the coffins filled by that older and real Terror—that unspeakably bitter and awful Terror which none of us has been taught to see in its vastness or pity as it deserves."

The Cost of Moderation

Fourthly, is there not implicit in the regret over the cost of revolution the idea that if there should be any changes needed in the status quo —when such a need is admitted—that these can be brought about gradually, moderately, and without fuss, as it were? But where one is dealing with really significant changes, policies of reformism, of gradualism, of so-called moderation, are in reality policies of acquiescence in the prevailing conditions. Have significant changes in the past come through polices of moderation? Is that how, for example, the United States came into being? Is that how feudal privileges were eliminated anywhere in the world? Is that how chattel slavery was wiped out in our own country?

There were advocates of moderation in the United States on this question of Negro slavery —of course, they were not among the slaves, themselves. To cry "moderation" is not difficult when it is the other fellow who is being crucified; especially if the other man's suffering represents enormous vested interests. But this tactic then would not do because it showed a failure to comprehend the nature of slavery—the fact that it rep-

resented several billions of dollars; the fact that
the class owning those slaves wielded on that
basis enormous political power; and the fact that
the way to end slavery was to end it, not "moderate" it.   Had the moderationists prevailed,
we would still be debating the question of slavery in this country, and wondering whether or
not it would be wise to pass a gradual emanci-
pationist act in the year 2612, to take effect, a
little at a time, perhaps, in 3200 *A.D.* And while
the rest of us were "patient" and talked and pon-
dered and wondered, the Negro millions would
be asked, of course, to go on enduring slavery.

Moreover, this moderationist approach views
the status quo as static; but a social organism, being an organism, will be everything except static.   It will be in process of change, and this may
be progressive or retrogressive.   One thing society is not, and that is static.   This tactic of
moderation ignores the tendency of those who
are dominant to seek to gain more and more
through their domination and to do everything
they can to make more and more secure their
domination.   The fact of the matter is that a
policy of moderation will not adequately serve
even to keep an exploitative social order from
retrogressing, let alone help in making any kind
of really substantial or significant progress.

Further, the moderationist, or reformist, approach, fundamentally accepting the status quo,
tends to shy away from any kind of mass struggle, any kind of significant widespread human involvement in the efforts to produce social change.
But the past demonstrates, I think, that nothing
is *given* by dominating classes, and this applies

not only to basic advances such as the elimination of slavery; it applies also to less fundamental alterations, such as the right to form trade unions, or the enfranchisement of women, or obtaining unemployment insurance. These accomplishments were the result of hard, prolonged, mass struggle; and to retain them and make them meaningful, after they have been obtained, also requires constant vigilance and mass effort.

We are not here arguing against reforms, but rather against reformism; the former are waystations on the road to basic social advance; the latter is the tactic of avoiding basic social advance. It is, of course, fundamentally on the basis of day-to-day efforts, on real questions having immediate significance for large numbers of people, that major social struggles occur. Accomplishments made in the course of such struggles prepare the way for other and often more substantial gains in the future. Further, the process of achieving such gains is a process of organization and education—in their own strength and in the nature of the resisting force—of the people participating, and in that sense also constitutes indispensable elements making possible the achievement of basic social advance.

The Cost of Progress

Fifthly, while we argue that those who hold that the cost of revolution is too high are profoundly wrong, we do not mean to indicate by this a belief that revolution is without cost. Certainly, it is not, and so drastic, prolonged and sweeping a development as is involved in the process of revolution will be costly. In it there will be human tragedy and suffering, some of it unavoidable, and some of it the result of failing and error and evil.

Great things are not come by lightly and are not achieved without cost.* But revolutionary movements represent profound human and social needs and forces; indeed, needs and forces that are irresistible. Fundamental to these needs and forces are the intolerable conditions emanating from the status quo, producing that mass awakening and activity without which revolution could not even begin, let alone succeed. Viewed historically and analytically, viewed realistically, and viewed in terms of the supreme end of existence—the ennoblement of human life—the record shows, I think, that the revolutionary process does not come at too high a cost, but rather as a breath of fresh air and as a force moving forward decisively the whole human race.

---

*Contrasted with the great severity of judgment concerning the socialist revolutions of the present century common among non-Marxist historians is the generally very considerate and as it were "objective" judgments conventional when evaluating earlier revolutions. Typical is this from the *Columbia Encyclopedia* (2nd edition, 1950), concerning Cromwell: "His military skill and force of character are universally recognized. He met the task of holding together the gains of the civil war and the disharmonious groups in the Puritan party in what seemed the only practical way. This involved cruelty, force, and intolerance which were evidently alien to him personally" (p. 483).

8. Non-Socialist and Socialist Revolutions

A. Expropriating Private Property

What differences are there between non-socialist and socialist revolutions?

In the great revolutionary sweeps that have hitherto marked human history, prior to the appearance of socialism, with slavery being replaced by serf-bound landholding, and this by wage labor, the private possession of capital, and the intense development of industry in Western Europe and in the northern half of the New World, there persisted one common characteristic: in all of these systems, slave, feudal, capitalist, the means of production remained the private property of a small minority. In other forms of revolutionary change, especially those associated with colonial and national liberation movements—for instance, the founding of the United States, or of the nations in Latin America—while very significant political, economic, and social changes appeared, again one thing endured, namely, the private ownership of the means of production.

It is exactly this element, which had resisted change in all preceding revolution, whose transformation constitutes the distinguishing characteristic of the socialist revolution. In this respect, the qualitative change encompassed in the move from capitalism to socialism is more profound than that in the move from feudalism to capitalism, or from slavery to feudalism, in that it puts an end to exploitation altogether.

It is a fact, then, that despite all the great changes that have marked pre-socialist history for thousands of years, there remained the constancy of the private possession of the means of production. The ultimate, decisive repository of economic and state power lay in the hands of the possessing class (or classes) ; and the basic function of government was to secure this property relationship. Constant, too, remained the identification of ability with wealth, of propriety with property, of the masterly with the master, of being rich with being good; and, the opposite of all this also constantly prevailed—the poor were the incapable, the poor were no good (the very word, "poor" having two meanings) ; and vulgarity was the companion of poverty.

This meant, too, that in all previous revolutions, some form of accommodation was possible and was practiced between the propertied class coming into full power and the propertied class being removed from full power. That is, for example, with the elimination of slavery, the slaveowners normally, as in the United States, remained as a class of significant landowners, with all the power and prestige inhering in such a class. In such revolutions, compromise was the rule, once the shift in power had been consolidated, and coalitions developed, with the erstwhile rulers now in a subordinate, but important and respected position, and united in fundamental opposition to the non-propertied.

Further, in the accomplishments of non-socialist revolutions, the developing system which is to replace the outmoded one has already come into being: the successful revolution indicates the *maturing* of the new system to the point where it can eliminate the old class from its dominant position. That is, the system of capitalism exists prior to the overthrow of feudalism, and grows to the point where it can overthrow feudalism. Here it is not simply that the new revolutionary class, the bourgeoisie, has come into being; its existence means that *capitalism* is already in existence and is functioning.

When capitalism grows to the point where it finds the restrictions of feudalism unbearable and where it possesses the political and organizational strength to force a change, it does so. But that change, and the coming into political dominance of the bourgeoisie reflects an already existing social system, namely, capitalism. And now, with victory, the bourgeoisie uses the state to help advance its own interests, to help its growth and development. In this, normally, it permits the existence of feudal remnants and welcomes the persistence of aristocratic families; later, as capitalism becomes worldwide, and especially as it approaches obsolescence and faces the challenge of socialism, it actively sustains feudal elements outside its own borders, and attempts a revival of certain feudal values within its own borders.

In all these respects, the socialist revolution is different. The socialist revolution, in the sense of the elimination from state power of the bourgeoisie and the gaining of state power by the working class and its allies, is accomplished prior to the coming into being of socialism. The bourgeoisie takes state power from the feudal lords and then uses the state to further develop an already existing capitalism; the productive masses take state power from the bourgeoisie and then use state power in order to *begin* the establishment of socialism.

Of course, in both the capitalist and socialist revolutions, the revolutionary classes have come into being prior to the accomplishment of the revolution and lead in its achievement; but in the socialist revolution, the working masses, having achieved state power, must start from scratch in remaking the whole character and nature of the social order. The significance of this distinction is intensified when one remembers that the socialist revolution seeks a more profound transformation than any revolution that preceded it. It seeks, for the first time, to eliminate the private ownership of the means of production; it seeks for the first time to produce a social order wherein acquisitiveness and personal aggrandizement are not the dynamic components of the economy, but are rather hostile to the economy.

Furthermore, not only must more be done, but it must be done by a class which has not had the opportunity of acquiring the skills and knowledge of rule and of direction. In the move from feudalism to capitalism and in the victory of capitalism, the bourgeoisie already had the experience of functioning as economic and political directors and administrators; that is, the capitalists, when finally taking over state power, had had experience in participating in state power. They had developed cultural, technical and educational skills of a high order and so had the qualified leadership, in the necessary numbers, to serve as diplomats, economists, directors, leaders, teachers, statesmen of the new social system.

But the working masses, in gaining state power and seeking to start the remaking of the social order, in a thoroughly basic manner, must do so without having had positions of leadership in the operative levels of the preceding social order. And since the change now being sought *is* so fundamental, cooperation with the ousted class is not possible.*

---

*Much of the post-Revolutionary writing of Lenin is taken up with this question of administering the new state, of finding effective personnel, of overcoming the bureaucratic and tyrannical practices of the past, of discovering and developing effective motivations. All these retain immediate relevance; would that all his urgings and warnings had been more carefully considered! Some examples: In his notes for a report, written in October 1921: "Bureaucracy and red tape... check all your work so that words should not remain words, by *practical* successes in economic construction." Letter to V. A. Avanesov, Oct. 15, 1921: "Unless there is a personal interest, no damned thing will come of it. We must *find a way* to produce incentives." Letter to P. A. Bogdanov, Dec. 23, 1921: Lenin urges a severe battle against bureaucracy and its punishment as a crime, in order "to really cure this disease." Two other letters from this period are pertinent. Thus, to D. I. Kursky Feb. 20, 1922: "We managed to adopt the worst of tsarist Russia—red tape and sluggishness—and this is virtually stifling us . . ."; and to N. Osinsky, April 12, 1922, a veritable cry from the heart: "the deeper we go into living practice, distracting the attention of both ourselves and our readers from the stinking bureaucratic and stinking intellectual Moscow (and, in general, Soviet bourgeois) atmosphere, the greater will be our success . . ." In Lenin's so-called "Testament"—the letter to the Party Congress, Dec. 24, 1922, relative to the dangers from Stalin, who is "too rude"

It is the central nature of state power and the enormous tasks that the state must undertake in producing the socialist revolution that make the concept of the transformation of the nature of the state so basic a component of the political theory of Marxism. It is the extreme difficulty involved in developing a loyal and skilled administrative group, under these unprecedented conditions and for these altogether new aims, which accounts for the emphasis in Marxism upon the security of the revolutionary state.

Certainly, the basic distinction between socialist and non-socialist revolution, is that imbedded in the impact each has upon the private ownership of the means of production. One eliminates such ownership; the other modifies the kind of such ownership, but does not alter the basic fact that some form of private ownership of the means of production persists and that this ultimately controls the character of the other features of the social order.

B. The Better Society

Socialist revolution, unlike its predecessors, being based upon what its adherents consider to be a scientific world outlook—dialectical materialism—signifies a higher level of consciousness in the struggle to achieve it, and a policy of

---

and not sufficiently "tolerant," "polite," "considerate," and Trotsky, who "has displayed excessive self-assurance and shown excessive preoccupation with the purely administrative side of work"—one finds again this emphasis upon bureaucratic perils. (See V. I. Lenin, *Collected Works*, Vol. 36, Progress Publishers, Moscow, 1966)

consistent planning in the effort to safeguard it and to build a new society.

Socialist revolution conceives of itself as instituting a system wherein dynamics, change, being an immutable law, continues to function. Unlike preceding revolutions, this one does not view itself as being the last. The socialist revolution does lay the groundwork for the appearance of a social order without class antagonisms, the resolving of which, hitherto, comprised the main force propelling change; but replacing this, under socialism, appear the perpetual drive toward the fuller and fuller conquest of nature, and also the process of criticism and self-criticism. These forces will, with sufficient technological advances, make certain the development of communism out of socialism, with the former differing from the latter in the assurance of abundance for all, in the presence of a general equalitarianism, and in the absence of institutionalized restraints having the character of the present state.

The socialist revolution brings into being, for the first time, a society opposed in principle to all concepts of elitism, whether this be based upon race or religion or occupation. The principle of service conquering that of aggrandizement, this denial of elitism will apply also to varying endowments of talent or capacity, in which, if there be real superiority, it will require enhanced contributions and service, rather than gain enhanced reward and power. Furthermore, in a society marked by an absence of class antagonism and the outlawry of exploitation, the whole concept of leadership, which classically has involved beguiling and deceiving, will alter to connote especially effective participation and genuine guidance.

The opposition to elitism shows itself in socialism most dramatically in principled opposition to racism, which is outlawed in all socialist societies. This carries with it not only laws and regulations for the society itself; it also helps determine the attitude of socialist societies to the whole system of colonialism, based as that system is, ideologically, upon racism.

Colonialism and racism, attributes of capitalism, mean in fact a condition of parasitism in which the imperial powers provide their home populations with relatively higher standards of living and (often) greater political rights, on the basis, in large part, of the deprivations suffered by the peoples held in colonial bondage. A notorious manifestation of this is the policy pursued by imperialism of inhibiting the development of industry in the colonial world, thus forcing the colonial peoples to be suppliers of raw materials and purchasers of finished products, and, in both cases, at prices set by the dominating power.

Socialism not only makes possible a much greater rate of growth in industrial production at home, without the intermittent crises that are organic to exploitative social orders; it also has no reason to inhibit the development of industrial production in other areas of the world. On the contrary, socialist countries are interested in the swiftest development of economic potential throughout the world, for this can redound only to their own benefit.

Hence, in the ultimate test of social systems,

their productive capacity, socialism is superior to capitalism. For while capitalism, in its final stage, in the present century, is marked by a notable decline in its rate of productive growth in the major countries, it is also characterized by a tendency to restrict the productive capacities of the so-called "backward" parts of the world. For, in large part, the "progressive" features of the economy of the imperialist powers rested exactly upon the "backward" nature of the rest of the world.

The socialist revolution has torn from the grasp of imperialism large areas of this "backward" world and has, in a matter of a few decades, transformed them into remarkably productive areas, challenging the "advanced" capitalist nations for productive supremacy. Simultaneously, it pursues a policy of actively assisting other areas —those not yet socialist—in their effort to advance themselves industrially.

Furthermore, since under socialism the contradictions between the socialized means of production and the individualized mode of appropriation, characteristic of capitalism, has been eliminated, it is a system which is unmarked by periodic economic crises, and above all, by the horror of mass unemployment. Again, on the basis of the elimination of this central economic contradiction and of the profit motive that goes with it, socialism is a system whose basic motivations are revolted by preparations for or the waging of war. While increasingly, the economies of the advanced capitalist countries are maintained on the basis of enormous expenditures for weapons of destruction, and while such expenditure represents the most lucrative business there is, in socialism these expenditures represent pure waste. Far from the economic system of socialism depending upon war-making expenditures, they are fearful burdens to it.

Hence, the socialist system is characterized—and this for the first time in history, again marking a fundamental distinction between the socialist revolution and all revolutions that preceded it—by implacable and principled hostility to the whole phenomenon of war. As the truly cataclysmic nature of modern war is brought home more and more vividly to more and more millions of the human race, the fact that one system, capitalism, needs it and breeds it, while the other, socialism, detests it and struggles against it, enhances the revulsion against the former and the attraction of the latter.

The opposition to elitism of socialism also means that for the first time, this system actively seeks to universalize human knowledge and human culture. It insists that the great scientific and artistic treasures of mankind can be the possession of all mankind, and not of just a handful among the rich and the intelligentsia. From this surely will come in time not only the universal possession of these treasures, but also the creation of additional masterpieces on a scale never before approached by any social order.

On the basis of such mastery, and on the basis of a system of abundance and peace, the real and functioning sovereignty of the people will be possible; hence, with the socialist revolution the fullest implementation of the concept of government by, for, and of the people is made possible.

Note that in all of the above, none of the changes and advances come automatically or come at once. All must be actively sought after, in a planned and organized manner, and all will take not only much effort but also much time to achieve. Impeding will be not only non-socialist societies, but also the vestiges of the past within the socialist societies, some of these vestiges going back thousands of years, to pre-capitalist and pre-feudal times, such as the attitude of male supremacy, to cite but one example.

The conscious character of the socialist revolution, and the enormous problems of its achievement and safeguarding require a political party of a new type. This party of like-minded men and women, guided by dialectical materialism, motivated by opposition to a system breeding contempt for Man and institutionalizing that contempt in racism and war, and inspired by the visions and the achievements of socialism, has the single purpose of realizing the latter.

Without the objective and subjective conditions making social transformation ripe, it cannot come about; at the same time without a party of the type just described, the change will not occur and will not be retained. The party itself derives out of the basic transformation; simultaneously it consciously seeks to hasten and guide that transformation. And it stays with the effort through fair weather and foul, through trial and error, through failure and success.

Parties have endured persecution and prosecution, have survived internal betrayal and corruption, have even, Phoenix-like, arisen again after the wholesale slaughter of their members. The persistence reflects need; the socialist revolution is a conscious one and therefore its leadership will be and must be dedicated, organized, principled and—with varying lapses of time—victorious.

The difficulties will be great, as befits the greatness of the prize to be won. But the elimination of the private possession of the means of production, and the commitment to the building of a socialist society, with the working class itself leading the construction of an anti-exploitative order, constitute the prerequisite for the development of the truly human epoch of history.

As for revolution, nowhere has its genesis been put better than in the four lines from the poem entitled "Revolution," by the Jewish poet, Joseph Bovshover:

> *I come because tyrants have put up their*
> *thrones in place of the nations;*
> *I come because rulers are foddering peace*
> *with their war preparations;*
> *I come because ties that bound people*
> *together are now disconnected;*
> *I come because fools think that progress*
> *will stay in the bounds they erected.*